The Gift of Seeing:
A Biblical Perspective on Ontology

J. Alexander Rutherford

ISBN-13: 978-1-989560-19-8

To contact Teleioteti publishing for information or to provide feedback, please visit us at **https://teleioteti.ca** or email us at **info@teleioteti.ca**.

DEDICATION

This book is dedicated to my son, Asher. I wish I could see you grow in your knowledge of God your Father and Jesus your saviour, but I am thankful that you are resting with them now. Of God's many gifts, I am thankful for the hope of the resurrection, at which time I am confident I will see your face again.

CONTENTS

ACKNOWLEDGEMENTS

There have been too many men and women who have helped form my thinking on the matters contained in this book to properly acknowledge them all. To select only a few, I am thankful for many conversations with Andre Roberge and James Hooks during my time at Regent College. My understanding of biblical narrative formed under the guidance of Phil Long has left a lasting imprint on my philosophy. I am indebted to Brad Copp and Fred Eaton for introducing me to John Frame and Cornelius Van Til, who are perhaps the most significant influence on my thinking. Finally, I am grateful for lively conversation with Craig Gay and the students in the 2017 ThM seminar at Regent College, which helped me to appreciate the unique contribution of Martin Kähler to biblical epistemology.

ANALYTICAL OUTLINE

I. INTRODUCTION

    A. What Is Ontology?

    B. Why Bother with Ontology?

    C. How Will We Study Ontology?

    D. The Foundations of Ontology

        a. The Preconditions of Theology

            i. The Surrender of Autonomy

            ii. The Humility of Faith

        b. The Possibility of Ontology

            i. The Non-Christian Dilemma

            ii. Biblical Ontology

II. PART 1 - THE PROBLEM OF CHANGE AND IDENTITY

1. CHAPTER 1 – ALL IS FLUX

    A. Pre-Modernism – The World of Reason

        a. The Pre-Socratics

            i. Heraclitus

            ii. Parmenides

    B. Summary of the Problem

2. CHAPTER 2 – HISTORY: EMBRACING CHANGE

    A. History: The Medium of Change

    B. Redemption: The Mode of Change

SERIES INTRODUCTION

His divine power has granted to us all things that pertain to life and godliness, through the knowledge of him who called us to his own glory and excellence. – 1 Peter 3:3

God has not left his people without help in the day of trouble—or in the day of prosperity for that matter. The Bible is God's gift to his people, revealing to them Jesus Christ and the salvation he has accomplished. But the gift of Scripture does not end in revealing our need for salvation and God's provision for it; Scripture is sufficient for the entire Christian life. In his first epistle, Peter tells us that God's divine power has given us everything for life and godliness (1 Pet 3:3, cf. 2 Tim 3:16-17).

In *God's Gifts for the Christian Life*, J. Alexander Rutherford unpacks how God through the Bible has given us what we need to live faithfully in his world. Each volume unpacks the Scriptural teaching against the background of contemporary culture and shows how the Bible provides a firm foundation for our lives. Each volume is intended to be short, around 110-150 pages, and accessible to the interested reader. The primary audience is theologically interested lay-Christians (Christians who are not in paid ministry and have no formal theological training), students, and pastors.

Part 1, the Christian Mind, will address the questions raised by philosophy and culture concerning the nature and possibility of knowledge and truth. Part 2, the Christian Scriptures, will provide an overview of the Bible and its content to equip the reader for a lifelong engagement with Scriptures and with the world Scripturally. Part 3, the Christian Life, will orient the Christian life towards culture and the church in order to show what it looks like to live a faithful, theological life. Drawing on the resources given in Parts 1 & 2, Part 3 will set forth a framework for Christians to engage intellectually with culture, life, and the local church in order to serve better within the local church context and so further God's purpose in the world.

INTRODUCTION

The fear of the LORD is the beginning of knowledge; fools
despise wisdom and instruction. – Proverbs 1:7

"All is water," the words of one of the earliest philosophers, Thales (c. 624-
546 BC). They were apparently his attempt to explain what the world really
is. For most of us, it perfectly captures the madness of the philosophers—
those who attempt to figure out the nature of our world. Such a claim seems
patently absurd. Thales proposal was creative to be sure—and knowing that
over 70% percent of our world's surface is water, it even makes a tiny bit of
sense—yet it failed in its simplicity to capture the magnificent variety of our
experience. He was not the first to propose a crazy idea. The German
Philosopher Gottfreid Leibniz (1646-1716 AD) thought the world was made
up of little minds: even a rock had thoughts! Is this all philosophy offers us,
thought games detached from real life?

A. What Is Ontology?

It is hard to deny that much philosophical thought has been this way, and the
pursuit of philosophical knowledge has often done great harm. One area
where this is particularly true is called "ontology." Ontology is sometimes
used interchangeably with "metaphysics" to describe the study of "*being qua
being*" (the explanation of which would require far more space than it is

worth).[1] Ontology has different connotations in different spheres of thought, often relating to categorization, that is, how things should be related, and the hierarchy of these relations (think: Animal – Mammal – Human – Nicole). I have found it helpful to summarise ontology as the exploration of two immensely important questions concerning our knowledge and its relation to the world outside of ourselves. The first question is the question of *what* exists: what is it that deserves the title "being"? Are they different degrees of being or does this describe all existing things indiscriminately? We will see why this question is important later. The second question is the question of what it means for a thing to be something: what does it mean to describe James as a "human" or a certain object as "James"? In the history of philosophy, this second question has been closely related to the first. At this point, you may be rolling your eyes, but I hope that the importance of these questions will become clear as we explore them throughout this book.

B. Why Bother with Ontology?

We will address some aspects of ontology in this book because knowing what God says on several key issues concerning ontology has profound implications for the way we think about doing theology and, more broadly, the way we think about the Christian life and ministry in the Western world. This will involve both deconstruction, showing how the Bible pushes us away from certain ontological positions, and construction, showing how the Bible makes several important affirmations.

Ontology is important for us because the Christian tradition, the reflection of God's people on Scripture for the last 2000 years, is deeply intertwined with ontology. The Scriptures are clearly not a philosophy textbook, and they do not go out of their way to discuss the sorts of questions philosophers have asked. However, Christians have long believed that ontology is closely intertwined with theology, and the history of philosophy has revealed that Christian theology has exerted a profound influence on the development of the ontologies of the modern world. Through its teaching about God and his creation, the Bible cautions us from embracing many ideas prominent in the history of philosophy and makes several important positive

---

[1] This is Aristotle's description of the height of philosophical exploration, described in the book we call *Metaphysics*. It means studying "being" without reference to anything that is said to "be."

affirmations relevant for ontology.

That Scripture has implications for ontology is not reason alone to study it; I do not believe that knowledge for the sake of knowledge is a worthwhile pursuit. However, because the theology we proclaim is deeply intertwined with ontology and because every facet of our culture implies an ontology, it is worth addressing ontology from God's Word to hear what God himself says about these pressing issues. As a result, we may just come to worship God for the brilliance of his creation. Moreover, we may find ourselves better equipped to think through the challenges raised against our faith. Finally, we may find ourselves thinking more biblically about the task of theology and its expression.

In the following pages we will neither answer nor even raise every issue discussed in the name of ontology. Instead, we will focus on several crucial issues to which the Bible has something to say. As we unpack each issue, it should become apparent why these issues are relevant for Christian theology and thinking Christianly in Western culture.

C. How Will We Study Ontology?

I have tried to give the reason for studying ontology, the question that remains is, how? In *The Gift of Knowing* (the first book in this series) I sketched some features of a Christian epistemology, or view of knowledge. In it, I argued that the Bible is our ultimate norm or standard of truth. In the following argument, the Bible and its worldview will function as our ultimate presupposition, the foundational belief upon which the rest are built. In *The Gift of Knowing* I also argued that God has revealed himself in his world and given human beings reliable minds and senses. Therefore, we will also employ reason and our experience of God's creation. Some philosophers, as we will see, have doubted that our experience can tell us anything about the real world, so we will revisit some of the ground covered in the previous book. Our study of ontology will, therefore, involve considering the world in light of the Bible using the faculties of knowledge God has given us. One last factor remains, us. Every endeavour to know is ultimately ethical, asking the question "what ought I believe about this?" For this reason, we must conduct our study with an appropriate posture of humility and submission before God. As the Covenant Lord of all who believe in him, and the Lord of all the creation, all human beings—Christians especially—are obligated to think as creatures, as those under authority. This will not be study of ontology "within

3

the limits of reason alone," as Immanuel Kant would have it, but ontology within the bounds of God's revelation.

D. The Foundations of Ontology

The Christian study of ontology is thoughtful reflection on knowledge, the objects of knowledge, and their relationships with one another performed in submission to God.

As we will see in the following chapters, the history of ontology is deeply intertwined with humanity's quest to have exhaustive knowledge of the universe. No single human being—nor the entire species for that matter—can know every detail of the universe, so philosophers took another route to exhaustive knowledge. They tried to identify that one thing (or the many most basic things) that explained everything. If they could not know every detail, they would discover the one general idea that explained everything. They called this idea "being," and ontology has often been thought of as the study of being, the study of the ultimate nature of reality. We will see that the Bible has something to say at this most basic point of ontology, so from the start we will set out on a different path than ontology has taken for the most part.

a. The Preconditions of Ontology

From the very beginning, the Christian is confronted with the truth that there is no single category by which she can exhaustively know reality; there is no "being in general," at least in the way the philosophers understood it. "In the beginning, God created the heavens and the earth" implies, among other things, that there are two distinct modes of existence in this world.[2] There is

---

[2] Some exegetes debate whether "the earth was without form and void" (v. 2) indicates that Genesis 1 describes God merely shaping pre-existing matter. My own reading of the text agrees that "God created the heavens and earth" introduces the whole section to follow (Gen. 1:2-2:3). However, it seems that by saying "God created the heavens and the earth," the author means more than just he "shaped" or "formed" them. Moses indicates that God is the originator or cause of everything. The following verses do not bother explaining how God brought the created universe into existence; it only details how God prepared the earth for humanity, his representative kings. This is supported by the fact that the creation of the invisible

Yahweh, the self-existent creator, and "the heavens and the earth," the dependent creation. Though we may describe both God and his creation as existing, or having "being," God's existence is remarkably different than that of his creation.

For one, the creation is a dependent or derived existence: it comes from and depends on God. God's existence, in contrast, is independent and underived (theologians call this aseity). God is necessary, in that he relies on nothing to exist and the existence of everything else relies on him; the creation is contingent, in that it only exists because God willed it to exist.[3] For this reason, "being" with reference to the Creator and the creature does not mean the same thing (it is not *univocal*). Our ontology begins with this acknowledgment: the Creator and the creature are distinct. However, contrary to the beliefs of many philosophers and theologians, the rejection of being in general in this sense does not endanger our knowledge of God. Furthermore, God's transcendence (his utter difference from us) is not transgressed by the claim that he is rightfully said "to be" as we are said "to be." These points, though brief, have tremendous implications not only for ontology but also for the way language connects with reality.

Cornelius Van Til used to illustrate the Creator-creature distinction by drawing two circles, one above the other, with lines between the two. The separation of the two circles indicates their distinction, but the lines indicate communication between the circles: God interacts with his world. Because of this distinction, a Christian ontology will abandon the search for exhaustive knowledge. Such knowledge is impossible. The question is then raised, is ontology even possible? If there is complete distinction between the Creator and the Creature, can we really penetrate to the world beyond our minds? Can we dare say anything about a totally distinct being?

---

world—including angels—is excluded from the discussion. I conclude, therefore, that "the heavens and the earth" is a merism: it means, God created *every single thing*. Then the narrative focuses on the thing in view, the earth.

[3] Necessary in this context means that it is impossible for God not to exist. That is, there is no conceivable world in which God is not present, for without God there is nothing—a non-world. Thus, to conceive of a *world* is to conceive of a world with God. Contingent means that we can conceive of a world where the contingent entity does not exist. It is possible to conceive of—indeed there was—a "time" when the created order did not exist, before "in the beginning."

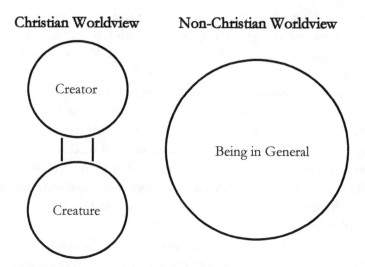

i. The Surrender of Autonomy

To these questions, the Bible gives a resounding yes—but by doing so it demands intellectual submission. That is, the Bible offers us the promise of true knowledge concerning God, our selves, and the world he has created, yet it offers them at a cost. The Bible is not a shopping centre from which we can choose the best bits and leave the rest; it is an all-or-nothing deal. If we want the answers the Bible gives us, we need to accept not only the truths we like but also the things we do not like so much.

The first thing taken from us is our pretence of autonomy. Reason is not our final authority according to the Bible; Yahweh is our final authority. He is supremely reasonable, in fact he is the source of reason itself, but his reason is above ours. That is, he has access to things we do not, so we will be stretched at times to accept things that we cannot verify by experience or logic. Indeed, we may be asked to accept things that *appear* to be contradictory.[4] If we accept God as our authority and are led to accept two apparently contradictory premises (i.e., God is three, God is one) on that ground, we can have the utmost certainty that the contradiction is only apparent, resulting from our finite understanding. Because of this, all our reasoning must proceed carefully in submission to God as he has revealed

---

[4] For more on this, see my book *The Gift of Knowing*. From the Bible, we can surmise that no biblical teaching nor feature of reality is truly contradictory, yet it may appear so from a finite perspective.

himself, primarily in his Word but also in his world.[5]

ii. The Humility of Faith

The second thing the Bible takes from us is our pride. According to the Bible we are not capable of submitting to God on our own, not in our actions let alone our intellects (e.g., Rom 1:18-32; 8:5-8). So to do this, we need help; we need to look outside ourselves.

First, we need redemption. Our incapacity is not a problem in our being (we are not metaphysically incapable) but in our hearts. We have all fallen short of the glory of God and willingly engaged in rebellion against him (Rom 3:23, 8:5-7). In doing so, we have earned his wrath, a verdict of guilty and the resulting punishment. We have continually hardened our hearts so that we would never choose to willingly obey him. God's answer to both these problems, and so the necessary remedy for our intellectual rebellion, is redemption through Jesus Christ.

Through the life, death, and resurrection of God the Son, Yahweh has enacted a New Covenant with all who are and will be his people. Of the many promises of this Covenant, one is the enablement of our hearts: God promised to his people in the Old Testament that he would one day do a work in the hearts of his people so that they would be able to love and obey him (Deut 30:6; Isa 54:13; Jer 31:31-34). He would take their hardened hearts of stone and give them soft, fleshy, obedient hearts (Ezek 36:22-27). By God's grace, we receive this promise (John 3:1-7; John 6:35-45); we receive the regeneration of the Holy Spirit and thus the redemption of our intellect in addition to the redemption of our souls. We are equipped by the Holy Spirit for obedient worship and life before God. This is the precursor to right intellectual pursuit, and thus a necessity for our adventure in ontology.

Second, we need illumination. When we are redeemed, we are regenerated; we receive that initial heart-change that enables obedience to God. Unfortunately, this initial work does not end all our problems. We sit in a tension between already being transformed and not yet receiving the fullness of what God has promised us. We still have the capacity, even the

---

[5] On the authority and difference of these forms of revelation, see *The Gift of Knowing*.

tendency, to rebel against God and sinfully warp his Word and commandments. However, we are not without hope, for the Spirit of God not only initiates our redemption and enables faithful thinking in us, but he also continues this work.

Illumination is a term sometimes used to describe the work of the Spirit in our lives to overcome our sinful blindness and sharpen our abilities so that we would grasp and respond to the Word of God (cf. 1 Cor 2:6-16, Rom 12:1-2). We need this same work to illumine our understanding of God's words in creation. Because of the moral corruption of the human heart, our theological endeavour has these two preconditions: we need to be regenerated by Spirit and continually empowered by him to appropriately receive what God has clearly spoken.

b. The Possibility of Ontology

Early we raised two problems, the search for knowledge of everything and the knowability of God. With these preconditions in place, we can turn now to the way the Bible enables philosophical enquiry and justifies—indeed, demands—knowledge of God. For the Christian, ontology is possible, but the non-Christian finds himself stuck between a rock and a hard place. Neither empiricism nor rationalism yields any knowledge of reality.

i. The Non-Christian Dilemma

For the empiricist, bound to believe only what he experiences, certain knowledge—even probable knowledge—is impossible. That is, knowledge concerns objects, events, and their relationships; we know the features of things and how those things will respond in certain interactions. However, to know any of these things, the empiricist must know every detail of the universe. That is, an empiricist may repeatedly observe a connection between an action (e.g. hitting a pool ball) and an effect (the ball rolling), yet he cannot say from his experience that there is a necessary relationship between the action and the effect. He has no experience of necessity, so he cannot say it exists. Even more problematic, he has only a limited experience of this relationship, so he has no reasonable ground to claim that this will happen in every circumstance. He cannot claim *to know* that hitting a pool ball will result in the ball rolling. All he can say is that he has the experience that thus far, hitting a pool ball will start it rolling. Regarding the ball itself, what could he say about it? He observes a certain colour, a geometric shape, 3-

dimensions, and weight. However, how can he know from his experience that this is not just a product of his mind? How does he know that there is actually a ball out there? Furthermore, given that he has reason to believe there is a ball, what can he know about this ball? He may know the above details, but he cannot know how the ball would feel in a different circumstance, how it would look in different lighting, or how it would react on a different surface. Indeed, he knows that as he moves farther away, he experiences the ball as smaller and if he gets nearer, the opposite occurs. Thus, it would seem that the size of the ball is conditioned by his mind, as is it colour—given that his colour-blind friend perceives it differently. If all he knows is his own experience of the ball, he really does not know anything about the ball at all!

He could spend his life with the ball and would not have exhaustive knowledge of it. Indeed, we may even question whether he has knowledge of the ball at all. The point is, even if an empiricist can gain knowledge of a particular thing, he cannot gain exhaustive knowledge of the universe. He cannot know from experience alone that another ball will have the same properties; he must then go on to investigate that ball fully. He must investigate every particular thing exhaustively to know everything. Such a task is impossible, so he is stuck with a very small body of knowledge, namely, his immediate experience.

The empiricist is stuck with limited experience of particulars and no knowledge of things in general (he knows a particular pool ball, but nothing about pool balls, or balls, or objects, or laws of motion). The Rationalist's attempt to exhaustively know everything results in the exact opposite situation. A rationalist will not use his senses to discern the details about a particular object but will seek to abstract from the particulars of his experience the unifying reality that lies behind it all. He moves from Fido, to pug, to dog, to animal, to living thing. The problem with "living thing" is that it is not at all helpful in understanding the particular "living thing" Fido: "living thing" tells us nothing about the features or character of this creature.

Going even further back, the Rationalist will arrive at "being," that thing which everything has in common. But what is being? If god, a dog, an amoeba, a black whole, space, dust, an imaginary flying spaghetti monster, or a cartoon on TV has "being" in some sense, what does "being" tell us? As Hegel observed, "being" is indistinguishable from "non-being": they are both empty terms! Because it must be infinitely flexible to cover every particular detail, it cannot have any details. Being itself is un-predicate-able; we cannot say anything about it. Yet, if we can say nothing about it, we cannot even say that it "is." The very postulation of a category "being" is self-contradictory, for to say anything about it is to describe it. If we cannot say anything about the thing that stands behind everything, what separates it from nothing? Imagine this "being"; if you remove every distinguishing feature of everything you know, what are you left with? You are left with nothing. Thus, the Rationalist seeks to know everything by coming up with an abstract explanation everything shares in common, yet the end result is no-thing—no knowledge at all.

ii. Biblical Ontology

The Bible brings us beyond this impasse. It does this in three ways; it qualifies the goal of ontology, it justifies the knowledge of the senses and the importance of particulars, and it gives us completely certain points of knowledge from which we can go about interpreting our world.

First, the Bible redefines the ontological task. Traditionally, ontology seeks certain knowledge of reality. Certain knowledge of reality must be exhaustive, so it seeks to come to know the essence of reality itself—being. Thus, ontology has been an end in itself. However, the Bible shows us that exhaustive knowledge of reality is impossible. The Creator-creature distinction indicates that there is no single point of knowledge ("being in general") that will give us knowledge of all things. Furthermore, we are shown in Scripture that we can have true knowledge of God but not exhaustive knowledge; even his thoughts are higher than ours (cf. Exod 33:17-23; Isa 55:8-9, Rom 11:33-36).[6] So exhaustive knowledge of the Creator is impossible.

What about the creature? The Bible teaches that there is an invisible realm beyond our experience, so a significant part of the created order is beyond our knowledge. There are spirits of all sorts, "Seraphim" and "Cherubim" (are these different or the same?), demons and angels, good spirits and bad spirits. We really have only a limited grasp of these beings and their abilities,

---

[6] Theologians will often say that we can "apprehend" God, grasp him with our minds, yet we cannot "comprehend" God, know him exhaustively.

for God has not chosen to give us much more than a glimpse. We know that they are active in our world, so our knowledge always touches upon the precipice of the unknown. However much we analyse and understand the regularities of our world, there are immensely powerful, personal beings active in the world, doing who-knows-what! Lastly, in the biblical picture of things, particular things matter, so we cannot have true knowledge without knowledge of particular things. We cannot, of course, know every particular created thing—even of the visible world—therefore exhaustive knowledge is impossible. What then is left of ontology?

For the Christian, ontology is not the search for "being in general." Ontology does not offer a way out of the difficult task of interpreting and living in light of experience. Instead, it is the exploration of the conditions of our knowledge that we might confidently engage in the task of knowing God and his world. Thus, *ontology is thoughtful reflection on knowledge, the objects of knowledge, and their relationships with one another that is performed in submission to God.* It is a fruitful endeavour because this knowledge is necessary for epistemology, knowing anything at all. It is particularly necessary for the sciences, studying the world in order to put it to use. It is also necessary for ethics, knowing how to act in and towards the world. In all these ways, it will aid us in the task of theology, applying the Bible in word and deed to our lives in the contemporary world.

Second, the Bible puts significant weight on particulars and so justifies the validity of experience for ontology. In several ways, the Bible shows us that particulars matter and validates the use of our senses to know reality. The Bible is not concerned with moving beyond particulars to a unifying idea; it places great value on particular objects and events. For example, "history" is not an abstract idea in the Bible, it is not merely the temporal flow within which the self-functions. History has a definite beginning, a definite end, and important moments that define it. That history has a goal means it is purposeful, meaningful; more importantly, the individual events of history have universal significance.[7]

---

[7] This is an important point, for in the Enlightenment, one of the most fundamental beliefs was the principle that the contingent truths of history cannot tell us anything about the necessary truths of reason. That is, historical events have no significance for knowledge and understanding reality. This is sometimes called Lessing's ditch, the claim that an uncrossable chasm separated reason from history.

We will consider this at greater length in Part 2, but consider Paul's words in 1 Corinthians 15: "And if Christ has not been raised, then our preaching is in vain and your faith is in vain" (15:14). If a particular event, the resurrection of Christ, did not happen, the hope for an end of history as we know it (the resurrection) is unfounded. The movement of history depends on this one event. Furthermore, a present state—namely, faith and hope—depends on the particular details of this event: Christ really must have died and he really must have been raised. Thus, a sort of abstract history like that proposed by Hegel (where the "resurrection" and other ideas are merely expressions of the idea of "freedom" working itself out as the world) is not valid. Particular details of the objects of these events also matter. It matters that Christ was physically present and physically resurrected. To Thomas who doubted, Jesus offered the evidence of his wounds; he said to him, "Put your finger here, and see my hands; and put out your hand, and place it in my side" (John 20:27). The reality of Jesus physical body (though resurrected) and the truth of his resurrection are here put to test by an empirical method. 1 John makes the same point:

> That which was from the beginning, which we have heard, which we have seen with our eyes, which we looked upon and have touched with our hands, concerning the word of life—the life was made manifest, and we have seen it, and testify to it and proclaim to you the eternal life, which was with the Father and was made manifest to us. (1 John 1:1-2)

See how John establishes the truth of his testimony about the Gospel of Jesus Christ and its implications: he emphasizes the physical nature of Jesus from sensory experience (cf. 1 John 4:2-3). Do not miss this: John appeals to sensory data for true knowledge of a particular object, the person Jesus Christ. He makes this appeal to uphold his teaching, his theology. In these ways, a mere sampling of the extensive testimony of Scripture, we see that biblical philosophy is interested in experience, that the senses do tell us about reality, and that particular events and objects are important. As we will see shortly, this focus on particularity without the loss of unity has immense significance. Because knowledge cannot dispense with particulars, we cannot have exhaustive knowledge of anything. However, because God, who has exhaustive knowledge of everything, has made himself and his world known, we can have true knowledge of somethings.

Third, the Bible gives us certain points of knowledge—unity and certainty—from which we can go about interpreting particular objects of our experience. If the biblical worldview is concerned with particulars, a comprehensive philosophy would be an exhaustive account of every detail of the created realm and God himself: it would be God's very mind. Unlike non-Christian ontology, knowing rooted in a Christian ontology does not search for exhaustive knowledge of everything. Instead, it is never ending growth in the knowledge of each thing: it is a way of life taken up by the individual. Ontology is, thus, not an end in itself but an invitation to wisdom, a framework to live our intellectual lives in submission to God and in the fear of him. A Christian is to interpret all experience in light of the Bible. Though we will pursue an ontology in this book, it will not be traditional "metaphysics," for we are not interested in those abstract questions such as knowing "being *qua* being." Instead, we are looking at how the Bible justifies and enables the Christian act of knowing; we are not outlining a particular individual's interpretation of reality—let alone God's exhaustive interpretation.

If experience were all there was, we would not be able to engage in ontology. However, God has not given us a world of "bare facts," or unrelated and meaningless things. Instead, he has given us a world infused with meaning, caught up in his plan for history, and revelatory of his glory and wisdom. The Bible is caught up in this dimension of knowledge, not just with things but with things *interpreted*, things brought into relation—even thought into existence (as we will see in chapter 9). Ontology is the study of particular *things*, the things that exist brought into relationship and thus interpreted. The point I want to make here is that the Bible does give us unity. The Bible not only justifies the use of our senses but also our minds. In Deuteronomy, Moses commands the people of God to love God not only with their actions and emotions but with their thinking (Deut 6:4-5). Further, Paul's writing is full of the use of logic (i.e. reasoning) and calls Christians to *think* about their faith and how they live it out (e.g. Rom 12:1-2, Col 3:1-3). The very fact that we have been given a book which is to be taught (e.g., 1 Tim 4:11-12) demonstrates that our minds are useful and thus to be used. Reading itself is a tremendous feat of reason. Psychologists and linguists in the 20th and 21st century have demonstrated the profound ability of our minds to naturally acquire competency in spoken languages. However, to read, to move from symbols on a page to understanding, is a far more complicated task, one that must be learned. Once taught, reading unlocks an untold world of understanding, but it is fundamentally a feat of reason, of our minds moving from meaningless symbols to a world of meaning through an intuited grasp of language. On these grounds, we are justified in using the tools of our minds and senses in the pursuit of knowledge, we may even find truth among the "rationalists" and "empiricists" who, despite their idolatrous use of these tools, nevertheless presumed upon their God-given reliability. We can and must use our minds and our senses, but we must do so only in submission to God.[8]

In addition to justifying the tools of our knowledge, the Bible also validates the physical/sensible existence of the external world. It likewise teaches us about an invisible realm which must be factored into our life, not only in our study of psychology and nature (e.g., Mark 5:1-6) but also ethics (oddly enough, 1 Cor. 11:10). It teaches us to be humble about our study and keep the particulars in view, but it also teaches us that there is an overarching interpretation of reality that we must consider. God exists, he has knowledge of all things. This means, first, that we must measure our interpretation of any particular thing by his interpretation of it; we must go to the Bible.[9] Second, this means that all events, and thus the objects involved in those events, must be interpreted in light of the broad narrative of redemption and its individual details (we cannot ignore the crucifixion of Jesus, his resurrection, the re-creation to come, the original creation account, or Noah's flood). Lastly, it teaches that God is actively at work in the world, intervening miraculously and consistently upholding it at all times. The body of this book will explore the conditions of our knowing, particularly in response to three challenges raised by the history of ontology.

This book is written for the interested—and potentially concerned—Christian, for those of us who have considered the worldviews around us and found them wanting or for those of us who simply desire to know more about the world God has created. Though we will be dealing with philosophy and philosophers, I will not assume a background in philosophy. I write to those who want to have an answer to the questions the world raises about

---

[8] I go to much greater depth on the content of this introduction thus far in my *Gift of Knowing*.

[9] More on this point in *Gift of Knowing*.

Christianity and who desire a more biblical way of looking at the world. By the Lord's grace I hope to point you to the treasure trove that is Scripture so that together we can be encouraged in our faith, be driven to worship of our heavenly Father, and be equipped to submit every thought to obey Christ (2 Cor 10:5).

Our discussion will be shaped around three significant challenges to the task of knowing raised by the history of ontology. The first is the problem of change, which we will explore in Part 1. The second is the problem of the one and the many, which we will explore in Part 2. The third is the problem of moving beyond the mind, which we will explore in Part 3. In each part, the first chapter (Chapters 1, 4, and 7 respectively) will introduce the problem by looking at several historical philosophers and their arguments. These problems build on each other, so there will be a natural progression from Part 1 to Part 3, moving from the early 1st millennium BC to the late 2nd millennium AD.

It is my earnest prayer that we would each come to see and truly believe that the fear of the Lord is the beginning of wisdom. To this end, I offer this prayer to the Lord for myself and for you, the reader,

> Father, you are the God who sees,
>   who looks on us in our weakness
>   and condescends to make yourself known.
> You have made yourself known,
>   and shaped us to know.
> Give us eyes to behold your glory,
>   hearts to submit to your ways.
> May we see with clarity the gift of your creation,
>   the intricate design of your revelatory work.
> In the name of your Son, Jesus Christ, Amen

Further Reading[10]

John Frame, *Cornelius Van Til: An Analysis of His Thought* [I-A]
John Frame, *The Doctrine of God* [B-I]
John Frame, *The Doctrine of the Knowledge of God* [B-I]
J. Alexander Rutherford, *The Gift of Knowing* [B]
Cornelius Van Til, *A Christian Theory of Knowledge* [A]

---

[10] The following resources range from (relatively) easy to quite difficult in their readability, I mark the easier reads with a B, those a bit more difficult with an I, and the most difficult with A. I adduce difficulty on the basis of both the depth of content, knowledge presupposed by the author, and the clarity of the writing. An asterisk before a book indicates that it is especially recommended.

—PART 1—

The Problem of Change and Identity

ALL IS FLUX

For God knows that when you eat of it your eyes will be opened, and you will be like God, knowing good and evil. – Genesis 3:5

For his invisible attributes, namely, his eternal power and divine nature, have been clearly perceived, ever since the creation of the world, in the things that have been made. So they are without excuse. For although they knew God, they did not honor him as God or give thanks to him, but they became futile in their thinking, and their foolish hearts were darkened. Claiming to be wise, they became fools, and exchanged the glory of the immortal God for images resembling mortal man and birds and animals and creeping things. – Romans 1:20-23

The Bible begins with God: "In the beginning, God created...." Moses asserts three realities here: first, God existed at the beginning, and therefore was not part of that which began. Second, the God who is not part of the creation acted to bring about the creation. Third, besides him there is a creation that had a beginning at the hands of God. These realities have far reaching ontological implications. Genesis 1:1 separates the Creator from creature and identifies God as independent and personal, as an agent of creation. It also identifies the creation as a dependent and finite existence; it had a beginning.

But shortly after creation, this foundational distinction was blurred by

God's creatures: the Fall happened. The Fall is profoundly ethical—a rebellion against God—and epistemological—humans making themselves the ultimate standard of truth. It is also significant for ontology. Not only do human beings think they have the authority to judge right and wrong and true and false independently of God, but they also blur the distinction between God and his creatures.

This is, of course, the lie of the serpent: if you eat, you will be like God. At the heart of the rebellion in the garden was the claim that there was something human beings could do to become like God. Now, likeness unto God is not impossible in itself: humans were created in his image; they are fitting representations of him. However, in this, they remain dependent beings, receiving this likeness as a gift. In the fall, Adam and Eve believed the lie that they could break through their dependence and exalt themselves to equality with God. In doing so, they followed the foolish pride of Satan, the original rebel, who was doomed from the start by thinking he could somehow exalt himself above the heavens and be like God. His temptation to Eve, "when you eat of it, your eyes will be opened, and you will be like God, knowing good and evil," is an invitation to join in his own rebellious attempt to exalt himself to God's place.

The whole human predicament can be interpreted in light of this metaphysical rebellion: the creature attempts in futility to exalt itself to the place of the Creator. This is immediately evident in Adam and Eve's descendants, who begin to imitate God creative activity for their own sake (Gen 4:1-6:7). This is likewise clear early in the book of Genesis, before and after the flood. After God wipes out the sinful human race, sparing only eight human lives from his judgment (7:1-7:19), Noah's descendants immediately resume the sinful project of pre-flood humanity and build a tower. "Come," they called, "let us build ourselves a city and a tower with its top in the heavens, and let us make a name for ourselves" (11:4). With the tower of Babel, creatures once again attempted to exalt themselves to the place of the creator.

According to Romans 1, this describes the human predicament: every human being has wilfully dismissed God's existence and exalted the creature to his place (20-23). Paul describes it as futility and foolishness (21): knowing full well that God existed, humans have sought to interpret and define their world apart from him. Early in human history, even today, this took the form of idolatry. Idolatry exalts an object of the created order—often a human creation—to the place of God, attributing to a lifeless object the praise and glory due to God. Habakkuk captures in his poetry the foolishness of this endeavour:

> What benefit is an idol,
>> that its maker would hew it,
>> a cast image and a teacher of lies,
> for the maker trusts what he has made,
>> enough to craft speechless idols.
> Woe to him who says to wood, "wake up!"
>> "Awake!" to a dumb stone.
> Is it able to teach?
>> Behold, it is overlaid with gold and silver,
>> but there is no breath at all in it. (Hab 2:18-19)

In the 21st century, on this side of the "Enlightenment," we tend to look upon such idol worship with a sneer, wholeheartedly agreeing with Habakkuk's indictment. Yet are we so different? Paul says that all humans have ignored the existence of the true God and exalted the creature in his place. Nowhere is this more evident than philosophy. Philosophers eschew the humility of the idol worshiper and, divulging themselves of external gods, make themselves to be god.

As the Triune Creator of the Bible, Yahweh, is the Sovereign Lord and Judge, wielding authority and control over his created world, so humans once attributed these attributes to idols. The gods represented by idols were said to control the harvest and give humanity instruction, to have authority over them and exert control. The modern person has not jettisoned the idea of an authoritative and controlling being. They have only begun to consider themselves that being. The German philosopher Ludwig Feuerbach (AD 1804-1872) may have put it most bluntly when he wrote, "the being of man is alone the real being of God,—man is the real God."[1] Feuerbach argues that "God" is nothing more than the idealized human race: humanity considers the perfections of humanity and projects this ideal into a new being

---

[1] Ludwig Feuerbach, *The Essence of Christianity*, trans. George Eliot (Amherst, New York: Prometheus Books, 2010), 230.

altogether. For Feuerbach and the philosophers who followed him, "God" is the ultimate idol, a human creation. Humanity itself is the true god; it is the ultimate standard of right and wrong and the only being that controls this world.

Though Feuerbach may have been the bluntest in this regard, the whole history of ontology attests this same idolatry. From the pre-Socratic philosophers (c. 7th – 6th cent BC) to Richard Dawkins, philosophers have continually attempted to explain the world without reference to God and have, in doing so, made themselves to be gods. The key issues in ontology that we will address arose in this way, putting humanity in the place of God. The first issue is the problem of change. The problem is not change itself (though this is difficult enough to explain), but the relationship between change and knowledge: if everything changes, how can we know anything at all? We will trace this problem across early Western philosophy before summarising it at the end of this chapter. In the following chapter, we will consider change as a positive aspect of God's creation. In Chapter 3, we will argue that we can embrace change without abandoning knowledge.

A. Pre-Modernism – The World of Reason

Though not much remains of the early philosophical writings, what we know is that philosophy began as a rebellion against Greek religion. Greek polytheism attempted to explain the events of nature—good and bad harvests, storms and disasters—and the twists of fate, such as a loss in battle, with reference to a pantheon of gods. There were gods of nature and human institutions (such as war and wisdom). Human worship could manipulate these gods to gain an advantage, and a failure to do the necessary acts would result in physical consequences. The religious milieu in which Western philosophy was born was much like the religious world from which Yahweh called forth his chosen people. As our God called his people to cast off idols for the true worship of Yahweh, the philosophers called the people to cast off the gods in exchange for the world of human understanding. Thus, they set off in the opposite direction from the one on which Yahweh was leading his people. From the city of Miletus, the first Greek philosophers rebelled against this arbitrary system of religion, this system that attributed change and stability in nature and society to powerful "gods." In its place, they attempted to explain the world through reason alone. Greek society had already rejected the living God for idols; now the philosophers rejected the idols for themselves.

a. The Pre-Socratics

If we were to try to explain the world today, we would probably start with our senses, analysing what we perceive and trying to arrive at valid conclusions. This was not the Pre-Socratic philosophers' approach; their words are, as John Frame puts it, "the language of a man sitting in an arm-chair, dogmatically asserting what the whole universe must be like."[2] They did not go out into the world; they drilled down into their minds. They asked themselves what best explained their experience.

Some of the earliest thinkers tried to narrow the world down to one substance or ultimate material that unified all experience—maybe water or fire. Aristotle identified their focus as the "material cause" of change, the single thing that remained consistent across all change—whether, water, air, fire, or something else. Others focused on the changing nature of the world. That is, they noticed that things appear to change: water moves downstream, furniture wears out, and trees grow. Yet this change was problematic. If the water in a stream is always moving or changing, how can the Euphrates be the same river one moment and then the next. The water, the most prominent feature of the Euphrates, is no longer the same after a moment passes; the stream bed is constantly changing as water flows through it; even the Euphrates' location changes over time. If the identity of the Euphrates is its qualities, then it constantly being replaced with a new entity: its water, soil, and even location is changing every moment. Similarly, its colour will change given the changing light and the contents of its water. The life it sustains may change suddenly given the influx of pollutants, and its temperature will constantly be in flux. It would appear that if something's identity lies in the qualities it possesses, "No man ever steps in the same river twice."[3] That is, at each moment a new stream exists, with unique qualities different from that of the prior moment. Consider the Theseus paradox. Imagine a ship that is in service for an exceptionally long time, let's call it the Theseus. As the ship is damaged in war and over its long years of service, it will need continual

---

[2] John M. Frame, *A History of Western Philosophy and Theology* (Phillipsburg: P&R Publishing, 2015), 53.

[3] This quote is attributed to Heraclitus by Plato in his dialogue *Cratylus* (402a); it represents his thought, though it may not be his original words.

maintenance. This maintenance may be very gradual, but timber by timber, we can imagine that the entire ship is refurbished. If not a single piece of the original Theseus remains, how can it be said to be the same ship that was first christened?

If things are constantly changing, how can there be any consistency to the world?[4] How can we really know what the world is? If every feature of the Euphrates has changed in the last 20 years, how is it still the Euphrates? If every cell in a human body has died over the course of someone's life, how is it the same person? The early Greek philosophers had two answers to this problem of change: either the world is wholly changing or wholly unchanging. They were what we would call "monists," they believed that the whole world was ultimately one substance (maybe water, or matter—whatever that is). Therefore, as monists, they sought to explain everything by one principle: this one substance was either always changing or never changing at all.

i. Heraclitus

One the one hand, there was Heraclitus of Ephesus (535-475 BC). Heraclitus taught that change was the ultimate nature of reality. He claimed that everything changes, yet this claim would eradicate reason: if everything changed, a person could not draw stable conclusions about anything.[5] For someone committed to reason like Heraclitus, this is an unacceptable conclusion. So he introduced another idea, a principle that he thought brought stability to the world. However, on close examination, his principle did not fix his problem. He suggested that all changes, so one must ask: does the principle of stability change?[6] If it does, it cannot provide the stability

---

[4] If we witness such change on the level of our observations, how much more change is going on where we cannot perceive it?

[5] If A equals B one day and A does not equal B the next, any possible conclusion could be drawn. More practically, if a house is a house one day and a horse the next, how can someone know the house? If a river is no longer the same river when you return to it, how can you possess knowledge of it?

[6] A few generations ago, much was made of the fact that Heraclitus and later Greek thinkers called this principle ὁ λόγος, "the logos." Some exegetes tried to argue that this idea of "the logos" as the ultimate principle of order in the universe stands behind the use of ὁ λόγος, or "the Word," in the prologue of John's gospel. However, in context, there is no sense of this impersonal philosophical idea; instead,

necessary for knowledge. If it does not change, then "everything changes" cannot be true; it does not explain the entire world. Furthermore, if the principle of stability does not change, how can we know that everything else is, in fact, changing? Heraclitus was struggling to explain how stability—the necessary condition of reason—and change—the way the world appears—could coexist. Reason led him to conclude that change was the fundamental nature of reality, yet this ruled out reason in the first place.

ii. Parmenides

Adopting the exact opposite approach was Parmenides (510-440 BC) and his (slightly) more famous pupil Zeno (490-430 BC). Parmenides argued that change was an illusion, that the real world is unchanging. Change, he reasoned, required something to move from being (e.g. "green") to nonbeing ("non-green"). Because non-being is a contradiction, reasoned Parmenides, change must be an illusion. "How is 'non-being' a contradiction?" you may be asking. Non-being does not exist by definition (it does not have *being*). However, the moment one employs the term to say anything, its existence is asserted. To say something that was once green is now red is tantamount to saying that "it *is* non-green" (or so thought many early Philosophers). "Is" is a predicate of existence; in Greek, "being" refers to that term. Thus, a sentence that involves both "is" and "non-green" asserts of the latter the very existence its meaning denies.

Parmenides' pupil Zeno is known for putting forth perplexing parables to prove that change is an illusion. One of his most famous asks us to consider a race between a turtle and a hare. "If we give the turtle a slight head start," he would ask us, "who would win the race?" At first, we would think that the head start makes no difference; the hare would win! "Ah-ha," Zeno would respond, "but that is impossible! You see, for the hare to catch the turtle, would it not first have to halve the difference between itself and the turtle? Would it then not also have to halve that distance? Again, would not that distance have to be halved?" That is, there would be an infinite number of steps the hare would have to take to cross the distance between itself and the

John identifies the speech of God by which he created the world as Jesus. John explicitly links his prologue to the Genesis account with his introduction, "in the beginning" (John 1:1, Gen 1:1), and goes on to draw out the significance of "the Word" as the one through whom and by whom the creation was created (John 1:3, 10).

turtle, thus it would never reach the turtle.[7] Now, this is ridiculous: of course the hare would win! Yet, if our experience (a hare winning) contradicts reason, it must be illusory. Zeno's parable was intended to show that all change involves such a ridiculous scenario, thus it must be illusory.

To explain the world, Parmenides argued by reason that changelessness or stability was the true nature of the world. However, in doing so, he not only invalidated all his experiences but also ruled out the possibility of reason. Though truth and the laws of reason are stable, reasoning itself (at least for human beings) is a temporal process: we think one thought after another. In a sense, knowing is change. When we reason, we move from not-knowing to knowing, from some knowledge to more knowledge. If all is unchanging, then the learning process cannot happen. A person either knows or does not know; they cannot come to know. Therefore, all acquired knowledge requires both change and changelessness: an unchanging standard by which something may be true and the reasoning process.

These early philosophers illustrate a key struggle in ontology, to balance change and unchangingness (or stability). Throughout Western philosophy, there is tension between change and stability. Some philosophers argue that reality is wholly changing or wholly stable, yet the most sophisticated approaches have sought to balance both change and stability. Doing so is a crucial problem in ontology.

B. Summary of the Problem

In the history of philosophy, many treatises have been written on the causes and conditions of change, but this is not our interest here. Instead, the problems raised by the Pre-Socratic philosophers that interest us are the problem of change and identity, namely, how can something remain what it is through extensive change. We illustrated the problem with the picture of a river that is ever-changing or a ship that gradually has every part replaced. If every quality of the things we experience can change, we must deny that such

---

[7] This presupposes that it is impossible to finish an infinite number of events: from whatever point you begin, an infinite number of steps remains between you and the completion of the infinite set—an infinite set being the infinite distance, or other variable, considered as a whole. But is this necessarily true? Is there no case in which an infinite number of steps could be crossed?

qualities are the ground for identity (something being *this* thing) or deny the continuation of identity altogether (assert that I, James, am not the person who began writing this sentence). If we refuse to deny identity altogether, we are left searching for another ground of identity. For most of the Western Philosophical tradition, this ground was sought in the "form" or universal. That is, though the qualities that distinguish me from you change, my "humanness" remains throughout my life. "Humanness" is itself unchanging. Perhaps, therefore, identity lays not in what makes things unique, what distinguishes James from Marty, but in that which unites them, the form.

If we follow this line of thought, a correlated vision of knowledge emerges. That is, if what makes me "James" is ever shifting, it is not really a worthy object of knowledge. What you knew one day is no longer true nor useful the next. Instead, what is truly important to know is that unchanging core that defines me, in my case, "humanness" (for Fido, "dogness"). Moreover, the possibility of *knowing* the qualities that characterize me is called into question. If by "knowledge" we mean to know something about something, and if such knowledge may be true or false, the shear changeability of my qualities calls knowledge into question. That is, to know the feel of a specific part of the Euphrates at 5:30 PM on Sunday the 7th of March, 2021 says nothing about the feel of river at any other point or at any other time. Thus, I do not know something about the "Euphrates," instead, I know something about Point A of the Euphrates at 5:30 PM, 7 Mar 2021. This is brutally specific knowledge that really tells me nothing at all. Moreover, if truth is defined—as it historically has been—as correspondence between a proposition (a statement of belief) and reality, this statement cannot be said to be true. That is, there is no correspondence at his moment because "Point A of the Euphrates at 5:30 PM, 7 Mar 2021" no longer exists at 12:59 PM, 8 Mar 2021. Though it may have been true the moment I thought it, it is no longer verifiable, for the original correspondence ceased to exist the moment after the experience was registered. It would seem, therefore, that any knowledge of particular things, namely, of the distinguishing and particular qualities of each thing, is fleeting. What I know or do not know is changing each moment and the next. Because of such problems, many philosophers in the history of Western thought have chosen to make "universal" or unchanging truths the real objects of knowledge. For Plato, the true objects of knowledge were the eternal Forms, which we will consider in Part 2. Aristotle defined these forms in a very different way, yet they were likewise the true objects of philosophical knowledge. Aristotle did not argue this; instead, he asserted that what matters most when we know something is the "what it is."[8] Accidents—variable qualities such as colour, location, dimension, number, etc.—are "obviously" not objects of "science," "for all science is either of that which is always or of that which is for the most part. For how else is one to learn or teach another?"[9] Without much argument, he assumes that the contingent, what may not have been, has no universal significance or relevance for "knowledge."[10] The history of Christian theology has been performed as a "science" in this sense, pursuing the universal truths of reason. One recent theologian defined the knowledge pursued by Christian theology as "eternal and necessary truths."[11] This set of problems, the continuity of identity and the possibility of knowledge despite change, will be the topic of the following two chapters. First, in Chapter 2, we will see that the Bible does not have such a negative view of change; change does not endanger the possibility of identity or knowledge. In that chapter, we will merely outline the facts of the matter, that change does happen and this ought not be a problem. Second, in Chapter 3, we will then seek to show how this can be, how we might resolve the problems of identity and knowledge given God's revelation in the Bible.

---

[8] Cf. *Metaphysics* Book Z (7), ch. VI.

[9] Cf. *Metaphysics* Book E (6), ch. II.

[10] "it is opinion that deals with that which can be otherwise than as it is." Metaphysics Z ch. XV, cf. E ch. I-II, Z ch. I.

[11] John Webster, "What Makes Theology Theological?," in *God Without Measure: Working Papers in Christian Theology*, vol. I, T&T Clark Theology (London ; New York: Bloomsbury T&T Clark, 2016), 221.

Further Reading

Gordon Clark, *Thales to Dewey:* [I-A]
*John Frame, *A History of Western Philosophy and Theology* [B-I]
John Frame, *Cornelius Van Til: An Analysis of His Thought* [I]
Ronald Nash, *Life's ultimate Questions* [B]

HISTORY: EMBRACING CHANGE

All flesh is like grass
and all its glory like the flower of grass.
The grass withers,
and the flower falls,
but the word of the Lord remains forever. – 1 Peter
1:24

And we all, with unveiled face, beholding the glory of the
Lord, are being transformed into the same image from one
degree of glory to another. For this comes from the Lord
who is the Spirit. – 2 Corinthians 3:18

In Chapter 1, we saw that change created a world of problems for the early
philosophers. To simplify things, we can say that they were faced with three
possible responses to the problem of change. First, they could deny that
change happened, in doing so, they would reject experience but exalt reason.
This was the approach of Parmenides and Zeno. Second, they could deny
that knowledge was possible, rejecting reason, and deny the continuity of
identity through time. This was an approach taken only by the most extreme
sceptics. Third, they could find a way to maintain change alongside of
stability, often exalting the latter at the expense of the former. In philosophy,
the changing world was treated as a lesser object of knowledge (if it was
knowable at all). However, the Bible would lead us in a different direction.
In this chapter, we will see that instead of rejecting either change or stability

or holding the two in an uneasy tension that favours the latter, the Bible would have us recognize the significance of the changing the world. The stability necessary for knowledge is not found apart from or in tension with change but is complementary to it: together they provide a holistic view of knowledge and the world. In this chapter, we will focus on change and its importance. In the following chapter, we will consider stability.

Let us start with the most basic of truths: the Bible affirms change. There was once a time when the creation was not, but "in the Beginning," God created it. However, God did not create it in an instant; he established it over the course of six days, with a seventh day rest. Even then, God did not complete his work: he commissioned humanity to continue his work of creating an earthly kingdom for his glory. Adam and Eve were entrusted with the task of populating God's creation and with bringing it under their rule, which represented his ultimate rule (Gen 1:26-30). Change is rooted not only in God's own activity but in the very nature of his creation. Moreover, God underwent a certain form of change in the process; he went from contemplating creation to achieving it, acting in a way he had yet to do. This was not the first movement God would undertake; he then entered his creation, enjoyed relationship with his creature, only to curse them for their disobedience. Later, he would promise himself to them in covenant. Then, when they broke that covenant, he descended as a man, "emptying himself" to become like his creatures to die in their place (Phil 2:5-11). Humans likewise change. Adam and Eve would have grown in their knowledge of God, each other, and his world if they had faithfully engaged in their God-given task. Instead, they grew in knowledge of each other and the world but became estranged from God. They were also cursed, along with the creation, with a sort of corrupting change: they would now die, have their bodies wither away and experience pain. In these ways, the Bible affirms *the experience of change*. We will consider in Part 3 how experience relates to the external world, but for the moment it should suffice to affirm that God and man change in their experience and that this is hardly a bad thing. Indeed, God wired change into the very DNA of his creation: it was designed to be developed, to grow. Moreover, this experience is not illusory. God grants experience an important epistemic status. In the early narratives of the Bible, we are not given any hint that the world of experience, with all its flux, is a bad or untrustworthy thing. This is affirmed as the story of God's world unfolds. When Christ becomes incarnate, he is experienced as the very revelation of God (e.g. John 14:8). It is not reason through which God is most clearly shown, but through the Cross: it is a single moment of the most vivid change—from glory to shame, life to death—that God is most clearly revealed (1 Cor 1:18-2:13; 15:1-11). When Jesus is raised, he does not offer philosophical proofs of his resurrection but his gouged side and pierced hands (John 20:24-29). As John reflects on his experience with Jesus, he recounts what he "has seen, and heard, and touched" (1 John 1:1-4). Sensual experience, taste, sight, touch, smell, and hearing are integral to the Christian experience of fellowship, ministry, and life together, both in communion with Christ and the saints. The Bible thus affirms experience, and experience is in its very essence change.

A. History: The Medium of Change

The medium of change is "history," the unfolding of events. The Bible is profoundly event-centred; it is not interested in the abstract truths of reason but the contingent truths of history. That it is, it does not offer abstract explanation for why things happen, neither impersonal and unchanging laws nor abstract necessities. Consider the creation; there is no necessity in the seven days: this is pure contingency, a choice God made. He did not have to do the work in a series of moments rather than an instant, let alone 6 days. He did not have to create man after the animals, nor a formless mass from which he would partition out the land and waters. The Bible gives no abstract reason why Christ became a man, such that this is the inevitable climax of creation. Instead, Christ's incarnation is presented as wholly determined and wholly contingent. That is, God's purpose in creation was to make known his glory through the demonstration of his mercy on the cross (e.g. Rom 9:22-24).[1] There was nothing accidental about the incarnation, crucifixion, resurrection, and exaltation (Acts 2:23-24, 3:18, 4:27-28). However, these events are themselves dependent on contingencies. Redemption was necessary because Adam chose to neglect his God given commission, letting Satan tempt Eve who in turn offered the fruit to Adam. The offering of God's own life was necessary because he chose to make a promise to Abraham, that God would take upon himself his people's covenant failure (Genesis 15:7-21). Jesus' death occurred at the hands of his own people, who

---

[1] Cf. J. Alexander Rutherford, *Revelation, Retribution, and Reminder: A Biblical Exposition of the Doctrine of Hell* (Airdrie, AB: Teleioteti, 2021).

chose to reject their shepherd and receive a criminal in his place. It was not necessary for them to nail him to a cross, but they did so, and in doing so fulfilled centuries of prophecy. Jesus' life consisted of hundreds of moments where he spoke, healed, and in doing so revealed his own glory and that of his Father. This is the grammar of Scripture: history.

History is the medium through which God has intercourse with his creation, covenanting, punishing, and rejoicing alongside of them. History is the medium through which God has made himself known. Whether in thunder and darkness, fire and smoke, a burning bush, a triad of men in front of a tent, or in the incarnation of his son, God has chosen to reveal his glory, his multifaceted character, and his enduring purpose through the medium of change. Change is, therefore, not something to be avoided. Events, because they are fleeting—here one moment and gone the next—are not to be shunned. Nor are individuals, because they change and pass away, to be ignored. Instead, individuals as the agents in events, which are the grammar of God's self-revelation, are the most important objects of knowledge. Knowing God in Scripture is knowing the agent (the person) who creates and destroys, who humbles and exalts. Knowing God means knowing the one who came in mercy and grace and who will return in judgment. Not only is the knowledge of God grounded in the individuality of history, but the community constituted by God's grace and love is radically individual.

B. Redemption: The Mode of Change

If history describes the medium of change, *redemption* describes its mode. That is, redemption is the eb and flow of history, the instrument by which the world is created and re-created and by which individuals are formed or destroyed. *Redemption* is not itself the goal of change but the means by which that goal is accomplished. Redemption describes what God is doing and what all other agents in the creation are doing in relationship to him.

When God created the heavens and earth, his commission to humanity was to build his kingdom. However, when humanity rebelled, a new reality emerged. No longer was the creation on a simple trajectory of unimpeded progress. Instead, two kingdoms were now at war. Those whom God had commissioned to create for his glory were now creating for their own glory. To build his kingdom, God would first need to redeem some of those who had fallen; indeed, kingdom building would now be defined in terms of redemption, the work of all of God's people to beckon those lost in darkness into the light and to then strengthen them in fellowship with God and one another. Thus, coming to know God, the expansion of God's kingdom, and the end of rebellion would be cast in terms of *redemption*, in terms of God's act to bring the lost to the light and to dispel the darkness. It is important to observe that the Fall and its corresponding redemption do not create change; instead, they dictate what sort of change must now occur. To attain glory— the fullness of God revealed and the perfection of his people—there must now be war and salvation. Redemption entails that change will not be from knowing to greater knowing alone, but also the changing of allegiance and the change from sinner to saint. Furthermore, God's people would always have acted towards one another and the creation, but now these actions are defined by the realities of Fall and redemption. They are acts not of neutral development but of healing and restoration.

The agents of redemption are not logical propositions or necessities but individuals. All changes involved in redemption are those wrought by and upon individuals. God is saving individuals to be a people for himself from the mass of individuals who are in rebellion against him. These individuals are not the faceless masses but certain persons with a unique contribution in God's redemptive purposes. Not all are hands or eyes, but each member has their own role to play in Christ's body so that his purpose in redemption will accomplished (cf. 1 Cor 12:1-31; Eph 4:1-14; Rom 12:1-8). Not only is change a necessary component of history and redemption, but the end of change is not itself changeless.

C. Glory: The End of Change

The end or goal of the change God has wired into creation is God's glory radiated among his people and a perfected creation. This is the end for which God has made the world and towards which redemption working across history will achieve. Change is not itself incidental to this end; it is change itself that accomplishes this goal. That is, if God forewent the complexities of history and simply created a perfected world, something would be missing, namely, the full revelation of his glory. The events and contingencies of history are the very means by which glory will be achieved. Far from being a problem, as the Greeks presumed, change is the meaning of the creation. It is through the give and take of human-divine relationships that God's glory is fully revealed. "What if," asks Paul, "desiring to show his wrath and to make known his power, has endured with much patience vessels of wrath prepared for destruction, in order to make known the riches of his glory for vessels of mercy, which he has prepared beforehand for glory" (Romans 9:22-23). Why did the fall happen? Because only through the destruction poured out on sin would "the riches of his glory" be revealed. Why has sin continued for millennia? That at the end of patience his "glory" would be revealed. I argue elsewhere that this passage points us back to the Cross, again connecting the contingencies of the crucifixion with the fundamental goal of the creation, the glory of God.[2] Or consider the book of Ezekiel, where the consistent refrain after every revelation of God's past and future actions is that "they may know that I am YHWH" (e.g. Ezek 6:10). So change is inextricably connected with the purpose of creation; the revelation of the glory of Yahweh, our God.

But will change cease when the creation is perfected? Once again, the answer would seem to be "no." The Bible offers no vision of perfection bereft of relationship, the intercourse of persons that defines history and which implies continual change. There may no longer be death and decay, significant forms of change that are characteristically negative. However, water will still surely flow, food will be eaten, vegetation will be consumed, experience will develop, and even knowledge will increase. We are not given an extensive vision of the New Heavens and the New Earth in Scripture, but we are shown enough to affirm continuity between this world and that. The characteristic nature of the future is not a lack of change but a lack of sin and its consequences, death and decay. The New Heavens and the New Earth are presented as the culmination of all that the earthly church pointed to, communion with God and man in the pursuit of his glory amid his creation.

D. Embracing Change

This is the first answer the Bible gives to the ontological problem of change. On the one hand, it affirms the reality of change with a resounding "amen!" Moreover, it does not reluctantly admit change despite its negative entailments; change is presented as fundamentally good, true, and beautiful. Change is what the creation is all about. Changes in knowledge, ability, experience, appearance, location, colour, quantity, and time are all

---

[2] See my book *Revelation, Retribution, and Reminder* (Airdrie, AB; Teleioteti 2021)

inextricably connected with what it means to be human and what it means for the creation to be all that it is. Change is something not only given to humanity but embraced by God in his communion with his people. Change is thus not a bad thing (a movement from being to non-being) or evidence of deficiency. Instead, change is a positive development in the communion of persons that develops what is already present, not filling in a deficiency but radiating excellence. The biblical view of change is not imperfection but perfection itself: perfection is the making known and exchanging the fullness of God's character shared with his people. However, if we affirm change in these various ways, must we abandon continuity of identity and the possibility of knowledge? Does everything merge into one indistinguishable mass of every moving thing which never experiences loss or addition?

Impassibility and the First Cause

Our argument thus far raises a significant issue in terms of classical Christian theology, which we will briefly address here. My goal with this book and all the books in this series is to argue by painting a portrait that is clearly dependent on God as revealed in Scripture, coherent with that revelation, and coherent with the world we experience. I intentionally do not engage with classic philosophy and theology at every point, for I think doing so is a futile endeavour that involves adopting the very presuppositions I am arguing are the problem. However, the issue of impassibility and its connection to Aristotle's causality argument is worth addressing.

A key pillar of so-called "Classical Theism" is the claim that God does not experience any change, including the sorts of changes I have attributed to him thus far in this chapter. There has been much written on the matter in recent literature, for and against the doctrines of immutability (God does not change), impassibility (God does not change emotionally), or simplicity (God is unmoved and unmoving, pure actuality with no parts). Though these doctrines capture some aspects of the biblical teaching—namely, that God is faithful and consistent, that he is not caught off guard or ever frustrated in his purposes, and that God is not dependent on a reality above or behind him—these doctrines are heavily reliant on the philosophical position we are criticising. That is, they presuppose that change is a bad thing or an imperfection. Because they assume with the early philosophers that change is negative, they can argue that God cannot change if he is perfect. We have already seen that the Bible never suggests that change is a bad thing. Several times the Bible affirms that God is unchanging in some sense (e.g. James 1:17), but it does so without ever denying God's actions in history or his "passions" (however we wish to qualify these). We will see in the next chapter that stability is an integral part of creation and central to who God is, so there is a very real sense that God is unchanging. He is unchangingly dependable, faithful, and consistent in his character. We can be sure that who he has revealed himself to be once is who he is today. He does not decay, grow weak, become feeble, or lose control; he is perfect yesterday, today, and forever. However, once we have jettisoned the assumption that all change is bad, none of these affirmations requires us to say that God does not change at all. God shows mercy, relenting from judgment he would otherwise have brought upon sinful beings. God responds with wrath towards sin. God created, revealed himself repeatedly throughout the creation, and became incarnate. Though God knows all things and is never learning new things, participation with the creation implies a sort of change in knowledge. God knew perfectly well that his Son would be crucified at a specific time on a particular day by specific creatures in a particular way, yet when the crucifixion happened, his perfect foreknowledge (this would happen) became perfect knowledge (this did happen). Such modal change is indeed change, but it does not imply imperfection.

Among the many objections raised against the claim that God changes, the most significant is perhaps the claim that God is pure actuality with the related first-cause argument. This argument dates to Aristotle but was most clearly articulated in Christian theology by Thomas Aquinas. On the one hand, it is claimed that for God to be perfect he must be pure actuality. In Aristotelian metaphysics, everything is a combination of potentiality (the potential to be something or have a certain property) and actuality, the reality of being something or having some quality. An acorn is potentially a tree; a green table is potentially a blue table; and a hot cup of coffee is potentially a cold cup of coffee. All change involves the move from potentiality to actuality. Potentiality is a deficiency or imperfection for Aristotle, for actuality is what all things move towards, potentiality being the possibilities of that thing being perfect. Accidental potentiality, such as colour, location, or temperature is also present in a thing: if a table could be green, then becoming green leaves open the potentiality that it could be red. Because accidents always imply potentiality, a perfect thing must have none. This leaves only the potential for substantial change, such as from an acorn to a tree. However, if a thing is moving towards its goal—if it still has unrealised potential—it is imperfect. God, therefore, as the most perfect being, must be completely changeless; it (for Aristotle's god is impersonal) must be pure actuality. Moreover, argued Aristotle and Aquinas, the created order requires a purely actual being to explain it. God cannot cause the world to come into existence directly, for he is unmoving (he cannot change in properties such moving from "potentially creating" to "having created"), but he can be the supreme end of all creation, that to which all things move (the telos or goal of creation). There must be, it is argued, an uncaused cause that stands behind all movement from potentiality to actuality.

The first thing to observe about this argument is that none of its claims are derived from the Bible. Therefore, if we have good biblical reason to believe God changes, then we are justified in dismissing the argument; we have seen that we do. But let's think about it further. Is change always from a negative state ("potentiality") to a positive state ("actuality")? It is not clear that this is the case. That my marriage will be seven years long instead of six years next year does not imply any qualitative difference (a negative-to-positive relationship) between these two lengths. The movement from "knowing it will happen" to "knowing it happened" likewise involves no negative-positive relationship. Moving from calm to righteous anger is only a negative movement if we presuppose that "calm" is better than "anger," yet this begs the question; we must first know that changelessness ("calm") is better to make such a claim. The Bible presents both calm and anger as perfect expression of God's glorious character: the change from calm to anger demonstrates that God's wrath is not irrational but a righteous response.

Second, it is not evident that all change requires an external cause, so it is not self-evident that the first cause necessary to explain physical change and the world's existence at any moment must be unmoving.

Moreover, it is not clear that all forms of causation would violate God's aseity, or independence from creation—that he must by necessity be unmoved. In the first case, Aristotle, Aquinas, and many others have assumed that all change has a similar pattern. That is, they have assumed that physical change (from hot to cold) and what we would today call psychological change (from one state of knowledge to another) can be mapped onto the same explanatory schema. They do not argue for this assumption, and there is no good reason to accept it. For example, I believe that all human decisions have a cause. However, the cause of human decisions is not a cause in the same sense that one billiard ball causes another to move. In the case of a human decision, it is arguable that the causality involved is both internal and external. On the one hand, the decision is caused by a crisis, a moment that requires a decision. However, by definition, a crisis does not determine which decision is made only that a decision is made. The internal cause that leads someone to make one decision and not another is not analogous to billiard balls. Essentially, the internal cause is character, the collected habits and dispositions that characterise the self and its embodied expression. Already, it is clear that all change cannot be explained in the same way, so the necessity of an ultimate first cause for the physical universe that does not have its own cause does not immediately mean that God is unmoving, as Aristotle would have it, for God may experience other sorts of change with purely internal causation. Now, as Hume argued (see *Dialogues on Natural Religion*), we need to be careful in applying our experience of causality to God. However, biblical revelation invites us to make a more significant comparison between humanity and God than Hume allowed. For human decision making, for acts of will, there always appears to be the factor of crisis or the moment that requires decision making. If we analyse it closely enough, crisis always seems to have an aspect external to us. That is, I might be faced with the choice to write a book, yet there are dozens of experiences that have led to the moment where I am faced with that decision. Though this would always seem to be the case with humans, it is not logically necessary that a crisis must always have an external cause. Indeed, God is presented in Scripture as freely creating, so there appears to be at least one moment of decision (to create or not) that has no circumstantial cause outside of God himself. Having taken away the external aspect of crisis, we can see from the analogy of human decision making how God could make an utterly self-caused decision. Given this possibility, the first-cause argument does not lead to the conclusion that God cannot change.

This argument brings us to the second consideration raised above; namely, it is not clear that all causation violates God's independence from creation. A frequent objection raised against the claim that God changes (even in a limited sense) is that any change in relation to the creation would make God dependent on the creation. For example, in 2 Samuel 24:24-25 David offers sacrifices to God amid a terrible plague. God is said to respond to "the plea for the land," and he averts the plague (v. 25). On the surface, it would appear that David's actions have caused a change in God. It is claimed that such change (from wrath to mercy; from one passion to another with the accompanying change in their expressed behaviour) would not only make God imperfect because of change (the argument we addressed above) but would also make God dependent on his creation and, therefore, less than God. That is, if the creation in some sense causes God to change in his disposition or behaviour, then the resulting state depends on God's creation. At first, this objection appears powerful—none of us want to be caught saying God "depends" on the creation! However, the objection involves equivocation on key terms. That is, the sort of dependence implied in this argument is not clearly negative. If God were dependent on creation in the sense that he needed something from the creation or that his existence depended on creation, this would be unbiblical and clearly wrong (e.g. Acts 17:24-25; Ps 50:12). However, this is not what "dependent" means in the above objection. That God is currently angry at me because of my sin, and so his disposition is dependent on my sin, does not mean that he needs me or that his existence is dependent on me. Instead, it only means exactly what it seems to mean: God is rightly angry at specific actions I have taken, and thankfully shows me mercy because I repent and trust in his Son. Indeed, unless we accept the two premises that 1) all change is negative and that 2) all change is the same, there is no reason to object to the fact that God responds to specific situations and has different dispositions towards different behaviours. Indeed, the Bible claims this on almost every page. The Bible declares that God changes in these ways, so we should believe it. Furthermore, the arguments raised against the biblical claims to this effect are not nearly as strong as is often claimed.

Further Reading

Craig A. Carter, *Contemplating God with the Great Tradition* [I]
*John Frame, *The Doctrine of God* [B-I]
*Rob Lister, *God Is Impassible and Impassioned* [I]
James E. Dolezal, *All That is In God* [I]
James E. Dolezal, *God Without Parts* [A]
Matthew Barrett, *None Greater* [I]
See my reviews of *All That Is in God*, *None Greater,* and *Contemplating God* on Teleioteti.ca.

3

CONSISTENCY: MIND AND IDENTITY

All flesh is like grass
> and all its glory like the flower of grass.
The grass withers,
> and the flower falls,
> but the word of the Lord remains forever. – 1 Peter
> 1:24

The biblical picture of change does not imply the cessation of identity nor the impossibility of particular knowledge, but is this mere naïveté? I do not believe this is the case. However, if we pursue an answer along the lines of the biblical vision of history, we must make certain sacrifices. If knowledge in the Bible is the contingent sort, knowledge of history in all its complicated glory, then we cannot appeal to abstractions (to the Forms or universals) as the anchor of stability amidst the sea of change. We will consider universals more thoroughly in the next part; for now we can say they are not the answer we are looking for. What is ruled out by the biblical picture thus far is a principle of stability that is abstract, such as the Forms, or materialistic, such as an unchanging world. The rejection of these two extremes suggests that we may benefit from investigating the opposite of both principles, particularity instead of universality and immaterial instead of material. We can picture this in the following way:

1 Material   2 Universality

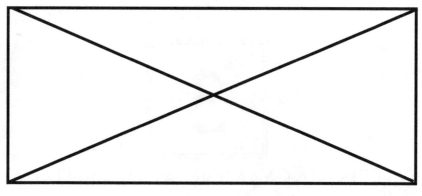

3 Particularity   4 Immaterial

Principle 1 is the claim that consistency derives from the stability of the thing-in-itself, therefore denying actual change. Principle 2 is the claim that consistency derives from a reality that stands behind multiple things themselves, the shared bit that never changes. If either is true, the other is redundant as a principle of stability. Principle 3 states that stability derives from the thing considered distinct from the universal shared by many things. Principle 3 is a possible interpretation of Principle 1, and if it is true, Principle 2 is false. Principle 4 states that stability derives from a non-material reality (a mental state or transcendent reality), not the material reality, which contradicts Principle 1. Principle 2 often implies principle 4, but not exclusively. The problems we considered and the biblical picture we saw in the last two chapters rule out Principle 1 and 2, thus leaving us with principles 3 and 4. If stability is rooted in the particular thing but not the particular thing as a material object, then we must take Principle 3 and 4 together. Therefore, stability is found in the particular things considered immaterially, which is another way of saying mentally. This can be viewed in two ways, subjectively and objectively. We will begin with the subjective perspective and then move to the objective.

Mind

The above argument does not rely on a particular view of the mind, only the rejection of physicalism. That is, we do not need to posit how exactly the mind is above the cause-effect world of the physical; all that needs to be conceded is that the "mind" is above matter. This is well supported by the cognitive sciences, which simultaneously demonstrate the interconnectivity between the mind and the body while illustrating the latter's relative independence. From the biblical perspective, we know that the self exists beyond the body's death, suggesting that the mind is not purely reducible to the body. Furthermore, the Bible indicates that humans are responsible and creative, able to make decisions and act in new ways. All these realities would seem to be an illusion if the mind does not transcend the body, for every "decision" would merely describe the subjective experience of a chain of physical cause-effect forces moving from external stimuli to internal neuronic processes. There would be no room for genuine "decision" making, where the subject acts according to a subjective force, such as desire. Moreover, the notion of "subjective experience" cannot be explained within physicalism.

Further Reading

Bradley L. Sickler, *God on the Brain*. [B-I]

A. Subjective Stability

If a stream has identity over time and yet its qualities are completely changed, then this identity cannot reside in the qualities themselves. However, there is another way to view identity. Individuals who view the Euphrates are not shocked by the changes they witness during their lifetime; they can still identify its continuity. Moreover, this continuity can be described in a book or orally, communicated beyond immediate experience. However, the consistent factor in each of these cases is an interpretation: a person has attached a name to an object of their experience and is able to describe and communicate that object to others. If the object itself is always changing, but it has a continuous identity, then the interpreting mind is the culprit. It is the interpreting mind which is responsible for creating identity. Identity is found in the particular thing, such as the Euphrates, but only in that particular thing as interpreted by a mind (see further, Part 3). We can see this working in the case of someone who loses their sense of identity, namely, their memories, relationships, and sense of continuity with the past or future. Even in extreme cases of dementia, the personal loss of identity does not entail the loss of identity in its entirety, for family, friends, and even doctors know the patient and interpret this person in terms of identity across time. They may also remind the person of his or her identity, which is recognized by others though eclipsed in his or her own mind. This identity is subjective because a person's experience of a river in the 19th century will differ from that of a person in the 20th century. They may not share any overlap in their experience. Thus, identity in this sense is *contingent*, variable from person to person. A man in the 4th century may have a concept of a river they call the ירדן and another in the 20th century of a river they call the Jordan, with no discernible overlap in their concepts. However, another person in the 21st century may correlate their own experience with that of individuals in the centuries between and develop a concept of the Jordan as it has developed from then until now, a single object which has undergone significant change but is identified by this historian as the same thing. Thus, we can see how the subjective identity created by an individual's interpretation can move towards an objective identity through communication. If we presume that the human mind itself is not subject to wholesale change such as we witness in nature, which is a point upheld throughout the Christian tradition on a firm biblical basis, then we can rightly maintain this subjective sense of identity (see the excurses above).

B. Objective Stability

Objective identity emerges once we acknowledge that humans are not the only ones doing the interpreting. We know from the Bible that history is not pure contingency; instead, it unfolds according to the foreknowledge and determination of God (e.g. Acts 2:23, 3:18, 4:28; Rom 8:28-30, Eph 1:2-23). God knows all that happens before it happens and works in his providence to bring all things to pass. Thus, there is no "bare fact," that is, uninterpreted thing. Every individual and aspect of this world is caught up in God's vision of and plan for the created order. God not only knows what I have done and am doing but also what I will do. He knows what I once was and will become. If the human mind can create subjective identity, then God's omni-comprehension (his grasp of all things) creates objective identity, an interpreted whole of all things as they are related, differentiated, and change across history. In response to the Theseus paradox, we can say that the shipbuilders and crew perceived continuity from one moment to the next.

THE GIFT OF SEEING

Even if they died with no overlap in their experience, God nevertheless perceived and determined the ship's fate from its origin to end. The identity of the Theseus is ultimately grounded in God's determination of history, though it is experienced and communicated from the perspective of those humans that have encountered it. The collective human perception of continuous identity, whether of a ship or a river, are like the pieces of a puzzle that fit together into a picture God has painted. Thus, admitting God into the picture offers us an answer to the problem of identity.

The interpretation of objects by humans and, ultimately, God not only provides an answer to the problem of change and identity but also change and knowledge. A full exploration of the later problem will have to await Part 3. For now, it will suffice to say that the biblical vision of change shows us that knowledge is fundamentally caught up with the particulars; God's interpretation of all things enables us to affirm this is indeed "knowledge." First, that objects have continuous identity despite change means that knowledge of any object concerns not only their present but their past and their future. Thus, the location and feel of the Euphrates on March 8, 2021 is not insignificant; it is one aspect of a broader understanding of the river as it has evolved over thousands of years. Second, it is true that there is no correspondence outside of the present for a proposition and the reality it describes, but this need not impede truth. We have already seen that interpretation plays an integral part in what it means for something to be a thing. In Part 3, we will see that this is truer than is presently apparent. Because interpretation is fundamentally part of what it means to know anything—moreover, because knowledge is always interpretation—and God possesses the perfect knowledge of all things, his correct interpretation of reality becomes the standard by which our knowledge is measured as true or false. That is, because all knowledge is interpretation, an object is an essential part of the act of knowing but not its sum. Therefore, it is unable to be the standard of knowledge. Such a standard must be the perfect measure by which knowledge is compared, thus a perfect interpretation. Because God possesses the perfected interpretation of all things, his pre-interpretation is the standard for our re-interpretation. All knowledge is, therefore, thinking God's thoughts after him. We do not, of course, have direct access to God's mind, but we can further surmise that God, desiring us to know and use our knowledge, has created the world and our faculties in such a way that we can reliably arrive at truth within the bounds of his spoken revelation.[1]

---

[1] See further, *The Gift of Knowing* (Vancouver; Teleioteti 2019).

—PART 2—

The One and the Many

4

THE RATIONAL WORLD

In Part 1, we consider the problem of change. This problem was prevalent in the period of the so-called "Pre-Socratic" philosophers. In the following centuries, Plato, his student Aristotle, and their heirs continued to address this problem. However, it was caught up in a more elaborate problem often called "the One and the Many," also known as the problem of individuation. In response to the problem of change, Western philosophy from Plato onwards has posited a two-world or two-principal schema for recognizing the reality of change while salvaging knowledge. On the one hand, there is the "One," the world of reason and unity. On the other hand, there is the "Many," the world of experience and particular things with all their differences. For Plato and those after him, the "One" was what mattered; it was the real world. The "Many" were the problem, and they were in one way or another subordinate to the "One." We will consider this problem in the work of Plato and Aristotle and trace it briefly across the history of Western philosophy until the time of the Reformation. We will then reflect on the nature of the problem.

A. Plato and Aristotle

The Pre-Socratic philosophers we considered in Chapter 1 were monists, that is, they try to answer the question of what is (of what exists) by positing a single explanation for all reality: all is one.[1] For Thales, everything is fundamentally water. For Heraclitus, the fundamental reality is fire, and it is perpetually changing. For Parmenides, the fundamental reality is an unchanging, spherical thing. All these philosophers thought that a sufficient explanation of the world must reduce everything to their unifying factor: there must be a single explanation for everything. Heraclitus realized that one principle was not adequate to explain everything, so he introduced another principle in addition to pure change, the principle of stability. However, this idea was not fully thought out in Heraclitus. Over the next two centuries, this idea of two explanatory principles was adopted more consistently by a philosopher named Plato and his pupil, Aristotle.

a. Plato

Plato (427-347 BC) may be the most famous philosopher in Western thought. John Frame observes that the greatest philosophers tend to take the seemingly disparate ideas of their predecessors and achieve a synthesis.[2] This is what we see in Plato. Plato's predecessors wrestled with change and stability, arguing that one or the other was the ultimate explanation of reality. However, we saw that change and stability are both needed to explain the world, to justify human thinking about the world. Plato brought the tension of change and stability together by positing two ultimate realities that explain the world. On the one hand, there is matter or "the Receptacle." The Receptacle is imperfect, featureless: it is responsible for change. On the other hand, there is the world of forms. The world of forms is stable (i.e. unchanging), perfect, and immaterial. The world of our experience is a marriage of the Receptacle, or matter, with the world of the forms.

The Receptacle, whatever it may be, is the principle of change in Plato's metaphysic. Change for the Greek philosopher's is a sign of imperfection: it implies moving from a negative state (not being, not knowing) to a positive one (being, knowing). The Receptacle is able to change into something

---

[1] At this time, there was another group of thinkers called atomists who explained reality as consisting of indivisible entities called *atoms* ("atom" meaning indivisible). Atomism is form of pluralism, the belief that reality is not fundamentally one (as in monism) but fundamentally a plurality. We will not consider this view further, yet it is interesting to observe that atomism and monism are two manifestations of the problem of *the one and the many*, which we will consider here.

[2] In, *A History of Western Philosophy and Theology*.

meaningful—the sensible world—yet it resists perfection by nature. The world as we know it is not the Receptacle; it is the Receptacle shaped by the forms. The Receptacle itself is featureless (pure change) and thus unknowable. Yet we only experience it as a crude resemblance of the perfect world of the forms, as a shadow resembles the object casting it. Therefore, knowledge comes not by looking at the things we sense but by contemplating the perfect world, which gives the Receptacle meaning. This world is the world of the Forms.

The world of the Forms is rather odd to wrap our minds around. It is immaterial, so above this physical world, and contains the perfect ideas of the objects (such as trees) and concepts (such as justice, love, goodness). These ideas are not particulars; they are not the idea of *a* perfect tree, but pure abstractions. That is, they are the unity, "treeness," that particulars, such as individual "trees," share in. If you look out in the world and see various trees, you see particular objects: you may see an oak tree or an arbutus. More so, you may see the oak tree on the corner of Walnut St and Creelman Ave in Vancouver, Canada. This particular oak has a history. Yet, the specific arbutus and the specific oak tree have something in common, a "treeness."[3] *Treeness* is what makes certain things trees. For Plato, *Treeness* exists in the world of the Forms, independent of any tree. It is hard to find an analogy for what Plato intends, but one way to think of it is like a formula: any particular tree can be derived from *Treeness*, yet *Treeness* is not a tree. Treeness is a truly odd concept, for it is nothing like a "tree": because all trees partake of it, it is neither brown nor white, neither leaved nor un-leaved, indefinite in shape, size, behaviour, root structure, age, or medicinal benefit. In the end, it begins to resemble "non-being," nothing at all.

To illustrate what he intended, Plato used an allegory of a cave. Imagine being a prisoner shackled and facing the back wall of a dark cave. The only light you had shone from behind you and illuminated the wall before you. On this wall were cast various shadows, of a statue, of a jar, of a lion, etc. These shadows are like the particulars; particulars, such as a tree, are faint shadows of the Form's perfection. Finding your chains unlocked, imagine turning around and discovering that various objects are casting the shadows

---

[3] In philosophy, a noun or adjective with the ending "ness" refers to the unity that all the particulars of the noun partake of. For example, every good act partakes of *goodness*. *Goodness* is the standard by which an act is declared good.

you have known. You would know a statue or a jar in part from the shadow, yet true knowledge of the statue or jar is found not by contemplating the shadow but by looking upon the real objects.[4] For Plato, these real objects are the Forms. Thus, actual knowledge does not come from our senses, which sense the particulars, but by our intellect, which contemplates the Forms.

In Plato's ontology, we see Parmenides' stability and Heraclitus' change brought together. The world we sense is ultimately unreliable; it partakes of ever-changing matter or the Receptacle. It is unknowable. However, there is an unchanging world that lies behind this one; this world is knowable. In answer to the question "what exists?" Plato's answer is that the Forms are the most real of all things and all objects experienced in this world have a derivative existence, partaking of the being of the Form and the non-being of the Receptacle. In answer to the second question of ontology, "what does it mean for something to be a certain thing," Plato's answer is "participation." I, James, am a human because I partake of the Form Humanness; I am "individuated," made other than that Form and different from you or Aliyah by the Receptacle and its distortion of the Form's perfection. Because all that differentiates or "individuates" me from you is negative, is the distorting effect of non-being, the differences between you and me are not important as objects of knowledge. Instead, true knowledge is the Form's perfection. Therefore, knowing "James" is only valuable in as much as experience helps us to move intellectually towards the contemplation of the Form "Humanness."

Plato's ontology has had a profound effect on the Western World. Philosophers are still discussing the problems he attempted to answer, and some Christians today even see a return to Plato as the key to living faithfully in the modern world. Plato's ideas had a particularly strong influence on Christian philosophy, primarily through the post-New Testament Neo-Platonists. The most famous Christian Platonist was Augustine of Hippo (354-430 AD), a North African bishop. Augustine's main contribution to

---

[4] If you are wondering where the light comes from, Plato gave the Form of the Good a particularly prominent position in the world of the Forms. The Good is the ultimate Form, it gives meaning to all the others. As all the particulars partake of a Form, all the Forms partake of the Good. This illustration is found in *The Republic* alongside the related illustration of "the divided line."

philosophy is in the philosophy of history. But he also took a unique position on Plato's world of the Forms. Philosopher's call Plato a "realist," that is, he believes that the Universals or Forms have an extra-mental existence: they exist apart from any mind. Augustine was not a realist in the same sense as Plato; he expressed an early form of what would be called conceptualism. He taught that the forms (e.g., goodness, treeness, justice) were not free-floating immaterial ideas but ideas in the mind of God. The only way humans can know particulars, argued Augustine, is because God illumines their minds with his understanding of the forms. For Plato, and for Augustine nearly a millennium later, the forms existed apart from the objects of our perception. For Plato, this meant two worlds, a world of perfect changelessness and an utterly unknowable world of pure change. Plato's star pupil Aristotle also believed in a two-fold explanation for the world, yet he attempted to bring together these principles in a way that Plato did not.

b. Aristotle

Aristotle (384-322 BC) was a particularly sharp student of Plato—so sharp that he was the tutor of Alexander III of Macedon, later known as Alexander the Great! Aristotle took in many of Plato's ideas but reformulated them in what he thought was a more reasonable fashion. In his work called *Metaphysics*, he explicitly rejected Plato's external world of Forms.

Aristotle believed that there is one world, the sensible world we experience. Everything in this world is ultimately explained by two principles, form and matter. If you take a table, for instance, it has various accidental (that is, unessential) properties such as a black colour, 4 feet high, etc. None of these features makes it a table. What makes it a table is its form, yet form is not enough to make a table. A table is also made of *matter*. In the case of a table, its matter is wood. The wood would likewise consist of form and matter, the latter of which would be form and matter once more. At some point you arrive at a base or *prime matter* that undergirds all change and is not itself defined by form. Contemporary philosophers argue that Aristotle did not actually believe in *prime matter:* matter is never apart from form. Form and matter are always compounded. However, the basic point remains the same. Whether or not matter can be considered apart from form, it remains the principle of potentiality, that which remains constant even when one substance becomes another (such as wood to fire). *Matter* is one of two foundational principles in Aristotle's metaphysic. It is like Heraclitus's ever-changing fire. *Prime matter* for Aristotle is indeterminate: it is featureless, unknowable. It is no different than nothing (or in philosophical terms, non-being) except that it is the necessary counterpart to form. Because *matter* is non-descript, it could be described as pure potentiality: that is, it can become anything. Everything in our experience is partly potential because it partakes of matter and partly actual because it partakes of form. Actuality is the realization of form in something. An example sometimes used is an acorn: in a sense, an acorn has the potential to become a tree. As an acorn, it is potentially a tree; one day it will be an actual tree. I said earlier that Aristotle's metaphysic explained the world with two principles, form and matter. Pure matter, matter without form, would be pure potential: it would have no features. Thus it could become anything. Pure matter is fully changing and changeable. For Aristotle, matter never exists apart from "form:" everything that exists consists of matter and form, with one exception.

Aristotle's god is unchanging and thus has no matter; it is pure actuality with no potentiality. This god is sometimes called the Unmoved Mover. The Unmoved Mover is completely unchanging; it does not interact with nor is it affected by the world. In fact, it does not know of or think of the world. It has been described as "thought thinking thought." How, you may ask, does such an entity earn the title "Mover"? For Aristotle, the Unmoved Mover is responsible for all change in the world, for the transition from potentiality (matter) to actuality (form). The Mover does not achieve this by doing anything; instead, it is described as supremely attractive. Like a magnet, the Mover draws everything to itself.

To the question, "what exists," Aristotle's answer is only concrete objects. Things exist, not abstract definitions (humans exist; humanness does not exist, or only in a secondary sense). Everything has a form or essence, which explains what it is, and matter, which is shaped by the form into the multi-faced objects of our experience. A specific chunk of matter, "this" matter over against "that," differentiates one human from the next. However, when it comes to "form," it is identical across every human, animal, etc. Indeed, the "form" is what something actually is. In his book the *Categories*, Aristotle makes it clear that any object is always a *something*: everything is defined, as a *human, animal, plant, table*, etc. This is an important point for ontology. What makes each human, the form, is identical across all humans. Moreover, this is what they are.

Concerning "James," that he is a human is more important than the fact that he is a Canadian, born in the 20th century, 6 foot 3 inches tall, living in Australia, etc. These latter qualities are "accidents" that specify what human I am talking about but only exist in and around the "substance," which is "a human." If I want to know how to act towards an object, I need to know something about its accidents (its location, size, etc.). However, if I really want to know why it is the way it is and what is most important about it, I need to know the form. The important ontological takeaway from Aristotle is this: what fundamentally exists are "substances," definite things such a *human* or a *horse*. It is not right to speak of something that is a *horse*, for "horse" is the most fundamentally real thing about it. Moreover, the "universal" ("horseness") exists as that which has caused many particular things to be the way they are; it is that aspect that is identical in each of them. However, this universal is just this: the identity of all these particulars; it does not, as with Plato, exist in another realm apart from the particular.

We see, therefore, both similarities and differences between Aristotle and Plato. For both, form and matter are important; there are particulars and universals, the form that characterizes something (that oak tree is a particular; treeness is the form). Aristotle attempted to bring both of Plato's worlds together into one: form and matter (cf. Plato's Receptacle) do not exist in two separate worlds; they are found together in every object. Both thinkers move beyond their predecessors by explaining the world not with one but with two ultimate principles. Both Plato and Aristotle held to a principle of change (Receptacle/matter) and a principle of stability (Form/form). What unites them most is the very thing that makes them alien to our modern era. Both of them are concerned with particular things primarily for the sake of the universal to which they point.

B. Patristic and Medieval Philosophy

The state of ontology looked much the same for the following two millennia. In the years following Aristotle, Greek philosophy tended to seek harmonization between elements of Aristotle and Plato's thought. There were unique movements, such as Stoicism, but by the 4th century, Neo-Platonism was dominant. Neo-Platonism attempted to integrate the logic of Aristotle with the metaphysics of Plato, resulting in complex and innovative systems of thought. However, in terms of ontology, Neo-Platonism closely resembled Plato and Aristotle. Western philosophy stuck close to its

Hellenistic origins for many centuries.

Things began to change in earnest just after the Reformation, though we cannot be certain why. Around the time of the Reformation, something happens. The study of philosophy turns from looking through the world or behind the world to looking at the world. Ontology became less about epistemology and more about reality. In his paper "The Christian Doctrine of Creation and the Rise of Modern Natural Science" (1934), Michael Foster argued that this revolution came out of the changes wrought by the Reformation.[5] Specifically, he observed that modern natural science depends on a uniquely un-Greek idea, that matter matters. Modern science is built on the idea that the physical world is valuable in its own right; it is a legitimate object of knowledge. Foster asked what accounted for the introduction of this un-Greek idea and identified the source as the Bible, specifically, the doctrine of creation. For Foster, what makes particular objects important is contingency, the fact that they are not exhaustively defined by reason. They are not reducible to a single idea such as "treeness." For the Greeks, a particular tree reduced to "treeness" as the sum of its intelligibility: to know treeness is to know the tree entirely. But for the post-reformation world, the uniqueness of particular trees become significant. Foster's study displays sharp insight into the shift that happened, but the cause of this shift may be traced significantly earlier. Nevertheless, the Bible is still the culprit.

In the 4th century, when the Church Fathers were hashing out the doctrine of the Trinity over against the many alternate positions, they drew heavily on the resources of Plato and Aristotle, mediated at times through their Neo-Platonic followers. When it came to the Trinity, the clear tension of God's oneness ("the Lord is one"; Deut 6:4) and his plurality ("...baptizing them in the name of the Father, and of the Son, and of the Holy Spirit"; Matt 28:19) was tantalizing similar to the ontological problem of the *one and the many*. For this reason, the so-called "pro-Nicene" Fathers (those who upheld the creeds of Nicaea and Constantinople) used the tools of the Greek ontology to resolve this dilemma. For the Basil the Great and his contemporaries, God was one in the same way that the universal was one, despite its many particulars. In his letter *To Ablabius: That There Are Not Three Gods,* Basil's brother Gregory of Nyssa made this connection definitively clear. In

---

[5] M. B. Foster, "The Christian Doctrine of Creation and the Rise of Modern Natural Science," *Mind* 43, no. 172 (1934): 446–468.

response to the argument that we say James, John, and Peter are "three humans," so the Trinity should be identified as "three gods," Nyssa countered that this use of language is wrong. There is only one "human," properly speaking, the "human nature" in which James, John, and Peter all participate. In the same way, there is only one "divine nature" (though we cannot speak of it), so it is improper to speak of "three gods." This solution is ontologically loaded, drawing heavily on the resources of Neo-Platonism. Athanasius and Apollinaris draw a similar conclusion, using the related resources from their Philosophical background. The problem with this line of thinking (at least as it concerns the development of ontology that we are tracing) is that it is, on the surface, incompatible with biblical Christology. That is, like their Hellenistic predecessors, the "universal," the one nature, is what fundamentally exists. The "many," the particulars, only exist in order to realize or "instantiate" the one. Yet in the Bible, Christ is said to be "made like his brothers in every respect" (Heb 2:17), and he is identified as God (e.g. John 1:1; John 20:28-29).

At the council of Chalcedon (AD 451), over a century of Christological conflict came to a head. The council incorporated the language of Pro-Nicene theology, that Christ was "consubstantial" (the same *nature*) as God, and of the later Christological debates, that Christ was "consubstantial" with humanity (of the same *nature*). "Nature" in these phrases refers to the universal or the "One"; thus, Christ is on the same ontological plane as both the Father and the Spirit, realising the one nature of God, and on the same ontological plane as James, John, and Peter, realising the one nature of man. What is not evident in the discussion at Chalcedon is the realisation that this Christological claim stands at odds with the Hellenistic ontology employed up to this point to explain the Trinity and other facets of theology. That is, if the "One" was primary and the sole purpose of the "Many" was to realise the One in the world, to give it reality, then it made no sense to claim that there was a person—even one person—who realised two distinct (and in many ways, contradictory) natures. This problem became the source of dramatic tensions in the following centuries of Christian theology. As Christians wrestled with Christology for and against Chalcedon, they came to similar conclusions concerning ontology.

a. Maximus the Confessor

The debates following Chalcedon, extending from the 5th through the 7th centuries, saw significant developments in the ways Christians understood ontology.[6] Though several of the fathers in the 6th and 7th centuries could be considered for their contribution to these developments, I have chosen to focus on Maximus the Confessor (AD 580-662). Maximus was an Eastern Father who became incredibly influential in the Eastern church after his death; he continues to have significant influence today. I have chosen to focus on Maximus not because of his unique contribution to ontology but because of his influence throughout church history. He is also the 7th-century father I have studied the most extensively. His ontology is exemplary of the developments that occurred at this time.

Maximus depended heavily upon Gregory of Nyssa; like Nyssa, Maximus developed a sweeping ontological vision of reality. In one sense, the nature was a concrete reality with great significance, yet unlike Nyssa, the essence was not what fundamentally existed. Essence was highly significant, but in Maximus we find it separated from existence. Nature or essence was not the thing that was most properly "being." Instead, nature was something that defined a thing: it was one of the properties that inhered in or around a thing. If that is not clear, neither was he (nor his predecessors). However, if we think about it a bit, we can get his point. When I say, "James is a man," it is possible to understand "James" as merely a sign substituting for the subject "a human" (as Aristotle would have it). However, it is also possible to say that "James" is the sign describing a fundamentally existing thing, a "substance" of which "a human" is the most basic thing that can be said about this "substance." This substance, "James," is Canadian, 6ft 3in tall, and, most importantly, "a human." In such statements, no matter how important the claim "he is a human" is, "humanness" has been put alongside the other "qualities" or "accidents" that describe a thing. The substance is not the nature; instead, it is an indescribable something that gives reality to the nature. Thus, theoretically, such a substance could "uphold" or "support" not just one but two natures. Specifically, in the case of Jesus, the pre-existent Son who was always "God" took upon himself the additional nature "Human."

The significance of this move was not truly seen for several centuries. However, by severing "nature" from "substance," essence from existence,

---

[6] Zachhuber argues for these developments. See his book for the development of ontology post-Chalcedon. Johannes Zachhuber, *The Rise of Christian Theology and the End of Ancient Metaphysics: Patristic Philosophy from the Cappadocian Fathers to John of Damascus* (Oxford University Press, 2020).

the nature or universal was rendered superfluous, or at least this was the claim of several Medieval philosophers.

b. William of Ockham

Centuries later, William of Ockham (AD 1287-1347) argued that everything for which the Greeks and Christian philosophers needed the Universal could be explained solely in terms of the mental act of relating particulars. Thus, the "universal" was solely a tool of the human mind: all that really existed were particulars. This move was only possible on the foundation laid by Maximus and others, such that the particular thing, not the form it embodied, was what fundamentally existed. This shift to the particular initiated by the Post-Chalcedonian philosophers and brought to a head by Ockham is exactly what Foster observed in his reflections on post-Reformation philosophy. In this way, Christian Christology led to the ontological revolution Foster identifies.[7] At the end of the day, particular things in all their strange and variegated beauty were the basic objects of our thought and knowledge and the only things that actually existed.

For Ockham and many philosophers after him, the God of the Bible had an essential role to play in philosophy and ontology. However, post-reformation philosophy turned in an autonomous direction for the most part: philosophers sought to explain the world apart from God and his revelation. The Bible opened a door for innovation in ontology, yet non-Christian philosophy proceeded to cut off the limb upon which it stood. Ironically,

> If the reason upon which they relied had been in fact what they took it for, a 'natural' faculty bereft of the enlightenment of the Christian revelation, it could have discovered no truths not discovered by reason to the Greeks, and could not therefore have laid down the foundations upon which modern science was raised.[8]

The Christian doctrine of Christ and, as Foster argues, the doctrine of creation give value to particulars (what Foster calls "contingency"). Furthermore, by laying the groundwork for the abolition of the realist "One,"

---

[7] Cf. Ibid.

[8] Foster, "The Christian Doctrine of Creation and the Rise of Modern Natural Science," 450.

these doctrines also leave God as the only one who gives unity to all the particulars. Yet though philosophers unconsciously adopted the belief that particulars mattered, they rejected the truth that Yahweh's will ordered all the creation to various degrees. Thus, the Bible's influence was enough to change the trajectory of philosophy, yet it did not stop the philosophers' efforts to explain everything without reference to God and his revelation. The temptation to eat and be like God was too strong for modern philosophy to resist. We will see in Part 3 that this had catastrophic consequences for the modern world.

C. The One and the Many

In these ways, ontology today revolves around two quite different foci than Plato, Aristotle, and the Patristic philosophers. In the modern era, the primary concern of ontology has been scientific, understanding the world as it is so that we can use it. The other concern has been atheistic, arguing in such a way as to exclude God from the picture and to open the door for human autonomy, namely, the freedom to interpret the world and act in it as each person sees fit. The latter agenda is characteristic of so-called Postmodernism but is not altogether foreign to Modernism. Because this is the focus of ontology today, the ideas of Plato and Aristotle seem very foreign. They are not concerned with the sensible world, for it is not the true object of knowledge. They are concerned with the unchanging world that is somehow related to the world of space and time. Even though Aristotle thought that form resided in sensible things, knowledge did not concern a thing—a tree—for the sake of that thing; knowledge concerned the particular only for the sake of learning about its form.

Because of this epistemological focus, the primary concern of Plato and Aristotle is a problem known as **the one and the many**. This is, alongside the problem of change and stability, the second major problem in ontology. Philosophers are those who seek knowledge; they want to explain the objects of their thought or experience. Therefore, a critical question that is raised when a philosopher examines the world is, "How can I know anything? What about the world justifies me in claiming to know something?" The philosophers realized that to know something about anything, we must know something about everything. That is, no thought—be it about a tree or a virtue such as love—exists in a vacuum.

We know a tree in relation to other trees and non-trees; we know love in relation to acts of love and acts that are not loving. Knowledge is essentially relational in this fashion. If I want to have true knowledge about a tree, I must not only know the tree but other things as well: I need knowledge of brownness, the colour of its bark; greenness, the colour of its leaves; the sun, which illuminates it; the earth, which anchors it; etc. If I want certain knowledge, I must know everything. That is, how can I be sure I truly know a fact about the tree if I do not know that there is not something out there that disproves that fact? Maybe this unknown fact is that I am all that exists, and the tree is a figment of my imagination. Or, perhaps, what I think is a tree is a shape-shifting demon spying on me! That one piece of data would fundamentally change how I perceive the "tree" and what it is. Therefore, without knowledge of everything, it is impossible to be certain about anything. Because no human can know everything, knowledge would seem to be impossible.[9] Therefore, philosophers were left with two routes by which they could know something. They could either appeal to unity or plurality.

The universe we know consists—apparently—of both unity and plurality: we know of a wolf, a pug, a greyhound, and a bulldog (particulars) and of dogs (a universal). For Plato, Aristotle, and their heirs, the most important thing to know about anything was "what it is." It was thought that we know what something is by the process of abstraction: we abstract generalizations from the particulars we experience. Experiencing wolves, pugs, greyhounds, and bulldogs, I can generalize concerning each of these that they are "dogs." You would think that knowing that a pug is a "dog" would give more knowledge, but, in a sense, "dog" is a loss of information: it excludes the characteristic smooshed-face and stubby legs of the pug. It especially excludes the particularities of Fido, a specific pug. Plato and Aristotle, along with many others, thought that true knowledge of something was found in the abstraction: I know Fido most fully not because of his particular characteristics but because I know dogness. "Scientific" knowledge, the knowledge pursued by philosophers, concerns only "what" questions:

---

[9] The alternative sometimes taken in more recent times would be to define knowledge differently. Instead of certain knowledge, one can be said to know even if that knowledge later proves to be wrong, what matters is warrant or the conditions for making a legitimate knowledge claim.

That there is no science of the accidental is obvious; for all science is either of that which is always or of that which is for the most part. For how else is one to learn or to teach another? The thing must be determined as occurring either always or for the most part, e.g. that honey-water is useful for a patient in a fever is true for the most part.[10]

Thus, contingent knowledge (knowledge of what is but could not have been) is neither desirable nor useful. Furthermore, if knowledge concerns the "whatness" of things, and this is found through abstraction, it then follows that one knows the universe most fully if he can abstract to a generalization that encompasses everything. Everything is "being." "Being" represents pure unity: a concept so broad it encompasses everything.

On the other hand, one could try to explain everything by appealing to particularity, examining every feature of Fido. Fido is black and white, short, about 2 feet long, has a short tail, etc. These can be broken down further: blackness and whiteness, shortness and length all can be broken down until we reach an underlying plurality that explains Fido. If we have arrived at the most basic explanation of Fido, we could say he is made up of "atoms"—indivisible things.[11] If they are indivisible, they cannot be described any further (to describe something implies that it could be broken down further, explained with something more basic than itself). The ancient Atomists gave the "atoms" elementary properties that would, in combination, produce all known reality. However, the attribution of various properties to the atoms was utterly arbitrary. Moreover, the interactions between these atoms were completely arbitrary, meaning that everything happened by chance. If one went beyond atoms, one may arrive at pure or prime matter, about which "nothing could be said" if it were really the stuff from which all else comes.[12]

---

[10] Aristotle, *Metaphysics* Book E (VI), Ch. 2.

[11] The irony of modern physics is that they used the term "atom" for something that we now know can be broken up further.

[12] John M. Frame, *Cornelius Van Til: An Analysis of His Thought* (Phillipsburg: P&R Publishing, 1995), 73. "But if every particular, every individual, is his own law and meaning, his own universal [i.e. unity], then again there is no meaning. Communication is nullified, since every particular or individual is an autonomous universe. There is no universal, because everything, ever last particular thing, is its own universal." Rousas John Rushdoony, "The One and the Many Problem—The Contribution of Van Til," in *Jerusalem and Athens: Critical Discussions on the*

Such matter must be able to take on every quality (if it is to explain every feature of Fido, the Earth, and the Sun), so it cannot have any qualities.[13] Thus, we see that a pure abstract plurality ("atoms" or "matter") is meaningless or arbitrary, as is a pure abstract unity ("being"): to reduce everything to a unifying or particularizing principle leads to no knowledge.

Plato and Aristotle are philosophers who attempted to uphold plurality and unity. For Plato, the Forms give unity to the world and are themselves unified by the Form of Good. The ultimate plurality of the world is found in the Receptacle. For Aristotle, the forms (with god as pure form) and prime matter (pure potentiality) served these roles. Ultimately, neither thinker was able to hold both principles together: both form and matter reduced to meaningless abstractions; in the final analysis, they yielded nothing any average person would call "knowledge," nor anything the Bible recognizes as "wisdom." How the two principles could be related remained a tension in Plato's system, as it does in Aristotle's. Both attempted to explain their relationship. Plato mythologized about a craftsman who united the forms with the receptacle, yet the craftsman would introduce a third principle at odds with the other two. For Aristotle, the Unmoved Mover attracted matter as its final goal, moving it from potentiality to actuality. In my opinion, this is hardly satisfactory an explanation.

The problem of the one and the many is thus a key problem in philosophy: is unity or plurality ultimate, and if both are somehow mutually exclusive, how do they relate? If the "One" is ultimate, what is its relation to the many which resemble it? If the "Many" are ultimate, what do we make of their commonality? At stake is the possibility of knowledge itself:

> How is it that this seemingly well-intentioned search for truth leads up such a blind alley? Van Til's analysis is that essentially both [abstract unity and abstract particularity] are idols, and thus self-destructive. They are idols because they are the result of man's desire for an exhaustive understanding of the world, an understanding that only God can have. As is always the case in idolatry, we seek for an ultimate within the creation, and when we think we have found it, we discover

---

Theology and Apologetics of Cornelius Van Til, ed. E. R. Geehan (USA: Presbyterian and Reformed, 1971), 340.

[13] This is a contradiction, for to say "it has no qualities" is to give it a quality.

in due course that it is utterly powerless.[14]

[14] Frame, *Cornelius*, 74.

5

THE MANY: THE PRIMACY OF THE PARTICULAR

In the beginning, God created the heavens and the earth. – Genesis 1:1

And God saw everything that he had made, and behold, it was very good. – Genesis 1:31a

by him all things were created, in heaven and on earth, visible and invisible, whether thrones or dominions or rulers or authorities—all things were created through him and for him. – Colossians 1:16

"What if this whole question is a red herring, a diversion or pointless pursuit?" Thus was the shocking thought that I had one day after years of trying to understand the problem of the one and the many. For many years, a dear friend of mine had maintained that this was the central or at least an important problem of philosophy, a claim to which many agree.[1] Following Cornelius Van Til, he believed that the Trinity provides the answer to this problem: both unity and plurality are ultimate; neither have precedence over the other. However, after I had read the arguments of Plato, Aristotle, and

---

[1] See, for example, Adrian Pabst, *Metaphysics: The Creation of Hierarchy*, Interventions (Grand Rapids: Eerdmans, 2012).

others, I still could not understand the problem—let alone speculate about the answer. Moreover, in 4th-century Trinitarian theology, the Fathers seemed to emphasise the One over the Many, as had Plato and Aristotle, so the traditional doctrine did not seem to solve the problem—whatever the problem might be! John Frame teased me in the right direction with his claim that Van Til did not *solve* the problem of the One and the Many but eradicated it.[2] What then was the problem in the first place—so I could understand how Van Til did away with it—? Then it hit me, the "problem" of the One and the Many was the nexus of several metaphysical problems with which the philosophers wrestled. On the one hand, there was the problem of change: how do we understand identity across time, and how can we claim knowledge of a world in flux? On the other hand, there was the problem of experience: how could we claim knowledge or attain a rational, scientific understanding of the universe if all we have access to is the tiny slice of the world which we experience, and no assurance that this offers a bridge to the rest of the universe? To attain knowledge of everything or to have a rational understanding of the world, there must be something behind the flux of the world. We could call this something the "logos," that is, reason or rationality.

This rationality must be that which brings unity to the diverse world. If this "rationality" is to render the world intelligible, it must have certain features. It must be unchanging, otherwise it could not itself be an object of knowledge. It must also be abstract, not an individual, concrete object of experience. If it were individual or concrete, it would not give unity to all things. If this abstract, rational unity is what gives order and meaning to the world, then it must be the object of knowledge instead of the changing flux of our experience. This is the kernel of the problem of the One and the Many, the postulate of an abstract unity that explains everything. The pre-Socratics, Plato, and Aristotle all took the "One" in different directions, as we saw above. However, once the One is raised to explain stability and reason, a problem emerges: how does it relate to the world of experience in all its plurality? For Plato, the physical world "participated" (whatever that means!) in the One—the Forms and ultimately the Good. The One individuated itself with "matter," the corrupting non-being of the receptacle. Thus, the

---

[2] He didn't say it in such words, but that is what I drew from his argument. Frame, *A History*, 544.

particular is less than the unifying rationality. Indeed, the particular is a corruption of the universal! Particularity and experience were dubbed "opinion" and sacrificed on the altar of reason. For Aristotle, there is no abstract form existing in another world; instead, the forms are abstract formulas that shape matter in specific, concrete ways. Every horse is a horse because of "horseness," the unifying, rational cause that results in it being what it is. All that makes it "this" horse and not "that" one, its accidents (colour, number, place, etc.), is irrelevant to knowledge, for knowledge concerns that abstract, rational form. Again, particularity was sacrificed for unity. For thousands of years, the One triumphed over the many, but imagine a world without the "One." If every particular was totally isolated, on its own, and irrational, then thought itself is meaningless. I cannot know what any other mind might think—if there are other minds—for every mind is its own, distinct world. Every event is irrational and unexpected, so I cannot predict what will happen even in the very same circumstances as before. "Human" is an empty term that does not describe actual commonality between you and me; it is an arbitrary name that someone has foisted on us but adds nothing to the knowledge of you or of me. We find that even the limited experience we have does not qualify as knowledge: we cannot hope to know anything, let alone everything!

But this is all a far cry from the world of the Bible, is it not? The Bible affirms particularity in all its glorious strangeness, yet it simultaneously affirms reason. What if the problem is not really a problem at all? What if it is a red herring? What if the problem arises out of the systems of the philosophers and not reality itself? I followed this thought for a bit and am now convinced that this is the case. The "One" as conceived by the philosophers does not exist, nor the "many" as they perceived it. In his *Parmenides*, Plato presumed that if there was no univocity, that is, if an idea and its corresponding sign did not remain stable and unchanging, communication was impossible! Is this really true? As will see in this and the following chapters, this by no means follows. Related to this claim, Plato, Aristotle, and their heirs believed that language corresponded to reality, such that the existence of the term εἰμί ("to be") meant that "being" existed, in some sense of another. Is this really true? The philosophers all agreed that the most important thing to know about anything was its whatness, but is this true? Knowing that my wife is a "human" surely means something, but is it more important than knowing her past, appearance, character, personality, and present relationships (e.g. that she is married to me)? Furthermore, what does saying "Nicole is a human" really mean? Is the latter an abstract formula that explains certain features of her? Or is it a sign that draws a conceptual relationship between her and other things so that by contrast and differentiation, she might be known better? Moreover, is change really a bad thing? Is abstract, universal knowledge really more desirable than concrete, personal knowledge? Finally, can we really explain the world's past, present, and future in terms of necessity—of abstract definitions and laws?

The Bible claims otherwise: God has acted and continues to act predictably but contingently, as do the innumerable spiritual beings acting behind the scenes! We saw in Chapter 3 that we do not need an abstract, impersonal reason to explain the endurance of things across time; this can be explained in terms of persons interpreting the world. The Hellenistic "One" and "Many" are a sham, an idol of human reason raised in the place of the living God but failing in the end to replace him. In this chapter, I want us to consider "particularity" or the "Many" in biblical perspective, not as something to be explained away but as the fundamental reality of God's world. In the following chapter, we consider the "One" in biblical perspective, or the function of universality in knowledge and the corresponding commonality of particulars.

Thinking biblically, when we speak of the "particular," we mean individual things and the events involving them. A "thing" may be a person, a dog, or a rock, and an "event" may be an action they perform or something that befalls them—even a moment of internal change, such as coming to know or a change in knowledge (from future expectation to present reality, for example). It will become clear in Part 3 that "things" are more complicated than are immediately apparent. Still, we will presume the conclusion reached there: despite complications, there are genuinely things outside ourselves. The Bible does not have a category for the Greek "Universal": this does not necessarily mean that it is incompatible with such a notion, though I have argued and will argue in the next chapter that this is so. Instead, what is crucial to observe is that as far as God has sought fit to reveal to us, the "Universals" are not a big deal. For Christians, this should have great significance: that thing which the Greeks said was everything is, in God's opinion, nothing. Instead of the Universal, the Bible is interested in the particular. In this chapter, I want to draw our attention to three groups of particulars with which the Bible is interested: individuals, actions, and events (in the sense of history).

A. Particular Individuals

The Modern era could be labelled the "dawning of the self," for it is at this time that a hitherto unseen interest in "interiority," or that existential core that makes you you and not me, emerges. At least in terms of philosophy, the ancient world was far less interested in personhood than our age. All sorts of reasons could be raised for these developments. On the one hand, we are a hyper-individualistic culture and not communal (then again, did interiority or individualism come first?). On the other hand, the ancient philosophers were solely interested in "what"s and not "who"s: "interiority" is by definition accidental, contingent, and individual, not universal. The Greek and Latin terms we translate "person" (ὑπόστασίς, πρόσωπον, *persona*) did not refer to "person" in any modern sense but to the individual, the particular or the Many over against the One. Christian theologian Boethius famously defined a person as "an individual substance of a rational nature,"[3] Leontius of Byzantium, followed by Maximus the confessor, defined it as a "bundle of properties around the substance."[4] However, the focus on mind and personhood would seem to be a natural development of the shift to the individual we observed above.

The Bible has no word that overlaps significantly with the modern concept of a "person," but the lack of a term does not mean the lack of a concept. If a concept is a relation between particulars, as I will argue in the following chapter, then a concept may exist wherever there is similarity between particulars. I will use the term "person" to describe the overlap between three sorts of beings in the Bible, humans, spirits, and God.

We could identify various similarities between these three categories. For example, they all have a sort of transcendence over the cause-effect

---

[3] *Persona est rationalis naturae individua substantia*. Boethius, *Liber de Persona et Duabus Naturis*, ch. 3

[4] Zachhuber, *The Rise of Christian Theology and the End of Ancient Metaphysics*, 278.

materiality of this world. God is the creator and Lord over all the creation; spirits act in and on the physical world, yet they are invisible and possess powers that seem to transcend the regularity of the physical. Humans have minds, however we may understand that term: minimally, they are above bare cause-effect physicalism, able to genuinely reason and make decisions. Personhood involves this basic transcendence (which we will call "mind"), the ability to think upon and react to the physical world without being determined by its material processes. Related to mind is *activity,* the ability to cause change in other things, to act upon them intentionally, in a way that a rock may not. Some might argue that animals have both these qualities, but the extent to which animals possess mind is debatable, and the Bible does not present them on the same plane in this regard as humans, spirits, and God.

Humans, spirits, and God—"persons"—share the ability to communicate with language: they are the only beings in the Bible and in our experience able to do this. Though many animals share our ability to develop concepts, language enables us to refine and communicate concepts, as I am attempting to do here with the concept "person."[5] Persons are thus active, communicative individuals (as opposed to abstract ideas or universals) with minds. Furthermore, these and only these are portrayed as "spiritual" individuals, in the sense of relating to God in a certain way. God is, of course, God, so he does not "relate" to himself, yet his character reflected in his will is the standard by which all creaturely relating is measured, so he is by definition "in right relation to God." Creaturely persons are in right or wrong relationship according to this standard. More concretely, God does relate to himself in the persons of the Trinity. Spirituality and communication get at another element of continuity between "persons," communality. This is obvious for humans. For God, he relates to humans as their Father and even friend, and he presides over and communions with his angels, even Satan (Job 1:6-12, 2:1-6; 1 Chron 21:1, cf. 2 Sam 24:1; 1 Kings 22:19-23). God also relates to himself as Father, Son, and Spirit (e.g. Matt 26:42; John 17:20-26; Rom 8:26-27). How about spirits? They commune with God (Job 1:6-12, 2:1-6; Rev), worship God together (Deut 32:43 [LXX]; Isa 6:1-5; Psalm 97:7; Rev 5:1-14), and communicate with humans (e.g. Dan 10:10-21; Luke 1:19-20,

---

[5] Cf. Michael Polanyi, *Personal Knowledge: Towards a Post-Critical Philosophy*, First Harper Torchbook Edition. (New York: Harper Torchbook, 1964), chap. 5.

Heb 1:7, 14). Thus, "persons," as a concept capturing the relation between humans, spirits, and God, are active, spiritual, communicative, and communal individuals with minds.

Something interesting emerges from this concept of "person." The Father, Son, and Holy Spirit are not hypostases in the Greek sense of manifestations of a universal (an ontological concept we have rejected), but they are persons in the sense we have just developed. Moreover, God as he is one would appear to be a person in this sense.[6] That is, the Spirit, Son, and Father are all identified at various times and in various ways as "Yahweh" (e.g. Matt 28:19; John 8:58; 2 Cor 3:17-18), and Yahweh is the one God (Deut 6:4). Thus, Yahweh, our God, as he acts throughout the Old Testament does not easily resolve into any one person of the Trinity, yet he communes with humans and spirits, is clearly transcendent (possessing "mind" in the sense above), is the standard and reference point of spirituality, communicates, and is active. God as he is one, Yahweh, is thus drawn into a concept of person alongside the three Trinitarian persons, humans, and spirits. Thus, all the major players are in the Bible are persons: God is so in a profoundly mysterious way, three persons who are also one person. When we say that the Bible is concerned with particular individuals, we mean with persons.

B. Particular Actions

The Bible is not concerned with persons as "persons," with the concept we have just sketched, but with persons as they act and interact. As it concerns God, the Bible is interested in making him known through his words and his deeds. God acts for and towards his creation; in particular, he acts for the sake of persons. God acts for the salvation of his people and the judgment of the rebellious. God's rich interiority (his character or personhood) is revealed in both acts: through them, we come to know him. Created persons are not just objects of God's actions but are actors in their own right; they are ethical beings. God created humans to represent him in the creation, to rule it and shape it in a way that would reveal and glorify him. After the Fall, redeemed persons were charged with building God's kingdom in a new way.

Under the New Covenant, God's people are to be like him and proclaim

---

[6] Cf. Cornelius Van Til, *An Introduction to Systematic Theology*, In Defense of the Faith V (Presbyterian and Reformed Pub. Co., 1974), 348, 362–363.

his good news to all the world. Through these contingent actions, God covenanting with man and man obeying God, God's glorious purposes are fulfilled. Not only are obedient persons and their actions involved in God's purpose revealed in Scripture, so are the rebels. Satan plays an integral part in the drama of redemption: his rebellious actions matter, as do those of demons. They are foils to God's good purpose, fulfilling through their foolishness the revelation of his fullness. In addition, God often furthers his purpose through sinful humans, such as Pharaoh, Nebuchadnezzar, and Cyrus (Rom 9, Hab 2:5, Isaiah 45). The Bible is concerned with persons and their actions; persons and actions meet in events, and the linear development of events is what we call history.

C. Particular Events

We discussed history in Chapter 2-3; we will reiterate here that events, particularly those involving persons (therefore, the events in question are contingent occurrences), are the focus of the Bible. Is not the crucifixion at the heart of history? What more contingent event could we imagine? Jesus prayed that it might be taken away from him, yet this was the Father's will, and he submitted to it (Matt 26:36-46). It was the Father's good pleasure to "crush him" (Isa 53:10). The Jewish leader's intended it for evil, but God brought it about to fulfil his good purpose (Acts 2, 4, cf. Gen 51). Pilate wanted to release Jesus but submitted to the will of the crowd (Luke 23:13-25). The crucifixion was not logically necessary; it is not the sort of thing "science" or philosophy deals with. Nevertheless, it is of the utmost importance for understanding everything. It is not alone.

God created all things intentionally and carefully, including the scope of history. Throughout history, God has entered into covenants; these covenants have driven all human history. When humans have failed these covenants, God has responded for salvation and judgment. With these examples and more, we see that the most important things to know about history and the world are contingent. The world begins with God's activity, "God created," its end is consummated by God again acting, "Then I saw heaven opened, and behold, a white horse! The one sitting on it is called Faithful and True, and in righteousness he judges and makes war," "Then I saw a new heaven and new earth…. And I saw the holy city, new Jerusalem, coming down out of heaven from God" (Gen 1:1; Rev 19:11, 21:1-2) Judgment will come because humans have rebelled against God; they have violated their covenantal obligations. Humans are saved because Christ came, died, and rose again and so established a new covenant within which sinners are declared right and enjoy fellowship with God forever.

Particular persons, actions, and events are what Scripture is all about. In each case, particularity implies contingency, which is the domain of experience, not reason (though contingency is far from irrational). The Bible is thoroughly oriented to the particular; thus, the particular is primary. However, biblical particularity does not come at the expense of reason and unity. Only godless reason and godless unity are jettisoned.

6

THE ONE: MAKING SENSE OF ABSTRACTION

Forever, O LORD, your word is firmly fixed in the heavens. Your faithfulness endures to all generations; you have established the earth, and its stands fast. By your appointment they stand this day, for all things are your servants. – Psalm 119:89-91

In the previous chapter we saw that particularity is primary in the Bible. Earlier, I argued that the "universal" as conceived by the philosophers does not exist; we will take that argument a bit further in this chapter. However, for the Greeks, such a conclusion is devastating. If contingency is dominant, if it is what matters most, how can we know anything at all? If all is change and uniqueness, is not knowledge itself futile and reason an illusion? This may have been the conclusion of the philosophers, but it is not the conclusion that the Bible would have us reach. We saw already in Chapter 3 that God's pre-interpretation gives unity to the changing world; we will see in this chapter that his interpretation of all things combined with his verbal revelation in Scripture gives us access to the unity we need to interpret the world rationally. The rational unity of God's world is not the One of the philosophers; instead, it is caught up in the particular without abandoning itself to irrationality. We can see this in three ways: first, unity comes from the orderliness of God's world upheld by his faithfulness; second, unity comes from genuine similarities among the creation and God himself; third, unity comes through concepts, the perception of relations between objects of knowledge, whether the Creator or the creation. We will briefly address the first two senses of unity, for they are not that difficult. We will then spend the bulk of this chapter on conceptual unity, which stands in the place of the philosopher's universals and explains the mental process of abstraction.

A. The Unity of God's Law

Thus says the LORD, who gives the sun for light by day and the fixed order of the moon and the stars for light by night, who stirs up the sea so that its waves roar— the LORD of hosts is his name: If this fixed order departs from before me, declares the LORD, then shall the offspring of Israel cease from being a nation before me forever." – Jeremiah 31:35-36

He is the radiance of the glory of God and the exact imprint of his nature, and he upholds the universe by the word of his power. – Hebrews 1:3

"Contingency," as I have been using the term, means something free from necessity. That is, something is contingent when it could have been other than it is, when there is no logical or physical necessity such that it would be impossible for it to be otherwise. The philosophers held that there was a certain necessity present in the world such that we could learn about everything by studying the rational framework (or *logos*) that explains everything. They did allow for contingency, but this was relegated to the accidents, the unimportant data of experience. We have already seen that the Bible prioritizes the contingent things of God's creation, but I have claimed thus far that biblical contingency does not rule out *rationality*. We have good biblical reasons for believing that God has granted his creatures rational minds and created a world that has a significant level of consistency. However, we are not permitted to believe that there is a rational cause for everything or even most things. We are constantly confronted by the twin realities of regularity and irregularity, of necessity (or better, determinism) and contingency.

In one sense, the world is utterly contingent, for every single thing results from personal and unnecessary actions. On the one hand, human actions throughout the created history have shaped the world as we know it, as have the unperceived actions of innumerable spiritual beings active in this world. On the other, the creation itself existed because God chose to create when he otherwise could have not created; he also made it in a way that was pleasing in his sight, not unreasonable but not necessary either. A fine distinction between the contingent and the necessary breaks down at this point, for we do not think of God's will, his acting, apart from the rest of his character, which is good, just, true, and perfectly wise. So, though we confess that God freely chose to create (contingency), we also confess that this choice was rooted in his character, making the choice he made the perfect choice to make as determined by his goodness, justice, wisdom, and righteousness (necessity). A similar dynamic is evident in human decision making, where we genuinely make free choices, yet we never do so without the internality of our character: all our choices are shaped by our past and present, our character, habits, desires, and fears.[1] This is where determinism, or "contingent necessity" (to introduce a rather paradoxical phrase) emerges. The entire world as we know it is dependent on God's decrees, yet these decrees are not arbitrary, they are informed by his character and are shaped by his ultimate purpose to make known his glory.

We expect, therefore, that the world is *rational*, that there are reasons things are the way they are, even if those reasons are obscured to us. The world is rational because God is supremely rational. However, the world cannot be exhausted by finite reason, for we do not perceive the whole counsel of God nor the actions of all the persons active in this world. We trust that God perceives—indeed, decreed—this complex web of forces that produce the world past, present, and future and rationally comprehends all things, but we are not permitted to think that we can have such knowledge in this life or the next. Therefore, whatever rationality we may possess, is dependent rationality; it is rationality only up to a point. We can penetrate to the reasons of the world in as much as God has revealed himself and, above all, his consistency.

The physical sciences work because God acts in consistent ways. We are never told explicitly in Scripture that God will always act one way and not

---

[1] See further, J. Alexander Rutherford, *Prevenient Grace: An Investigation into Arminianism*, 2nd Revised Edition (Vancouver; Teleioteti, 2020).

another; indeed, this is false. God periodically acts within his creation in unexpected, unanticipated ways! Such are miracles. However, we are told that God "upholds" the world by his powerful word (Heb 1:1-3). That is, we are told that there is a regular way God maintains the world. Psalm 119 reflects on God's Law and his Word in general; verses 89-91 speak of God's "word fixed in the heavens," correlated with the establishment of the earth and the continuity of the created order. This reflects the Genesis creation account, where we witness God speaking the world into being with all its attendant order, such as day and night cycles. When speaking of the New Covenant Yahweh will make with his people, Jeremiah points to the "fixed order" of creation and states that as this is consistent, so God will remain consistent towards his people (Jer 31:35-36). Thus, we ought to expect a consistent baseline of orderliness to the created world that was fixed by God. Against this baseline, the actions of non-divine persons stand out, and God's irregular activity appears spectacular.

In this way, God's law (his fixed order for the physical world and his consistent character reflected in his revelation by which our actions and thoughts are governed) gives unity to the particulars of this world such that rationality is possible. The task God originally entrusted to humans, to subdue and rule the world would, seem to imply harnessing our abilities of reason, our ability to interpret, communicate, and anticipate the world around us.

God's law is only one aspect of the unity God has built into the creation. Law permits us to anticipate changes according to patterns of consistent behaviour, but behaviour and change always involve individuals. If no individual had anything in common, then law would be useless to us, for there would be no consistency in the objects to which the law might apply. I would know what is morally right, for example, in one specific case—that it is not right to murder Tim—but there would be no similarity between that act prohibited and any other possible act nor between Tim and any other possible being such that I could apply that same law to any other case. Or, drawing a physical example, there would not be any similarity between various pool balls, cues, or tables—let alone players—to know that my experience of one ball moving at time A is applicable at Time B. All reason requires similarity among the things of the world so that what is true in one instance can be extrapolated to others.

B. The Unity of Created Likeness

When God created man, he made him in the likeness of God. Male and female he created them, and he blessed them and named them Man when they were created. When Adam had lived 130 years, he fathered a son in his own likeness, after his image, and named him Seth. – Genesis 5:1-3

The Bible does not so much teach the idea of created likeness introduced above as presuppose it. For example, God presumes that there is sufficient commonality in the world for the case laws given in the Torah to apply in endless situations (e.g. Exod 21:12-14, 28-32). Indeed, all ethical teaching in the Bible presupposes this, such as the ten commandments and the New Testament epistles. What the Bible does teach is that God has created the world with sufficient likeness that his people may know him and his world. This is especially true for humanity.

There have been endless treatises written on the "image and likeness" of God in Genesis 1:26-27, but several points do clearly emerge in the context of Genesis. In verses 26 and 27-28, "image and likeness" and "image" are connected with God's commission to Adam and Eve, that they would "be fruitful and multiply and fill the earth and subdue it, and have dominion" (Gen 1:28, cf. 26). Thus, part of this likeness is the ability to do to a limited extent what God does, to rule and create. Our reasoning faculties, namely, our senses and interpreting faculties necessary to make sense of experience, must be sufficient for this task; this implies a likeness to God's own faculties for (pre)interpreting his creation. Genesis 5 draws a parallel between God's likeness granted to Adam and the likeness shared between Adam and his descendants. This original likeness between humans and God is carried on through the family line of Adam and is analogous to the likeness which Seth has to Adam. With Adam, Eve, Seth, and God, there is thus a concept of likeness, a relationship shared between them. It would seem that as we can know something about Seth by perceiving Adam, and about Seth and Adam by perceiving Enosh, we can know something about God by perceiving Adam, Eve, Seth, and Enosh, for each shares a likeness with God in a manner analogous to their likeness with one another. This conclusion is sustained across the Bible, where God reveals himself in terms of his creation and humanity in particular, thereby assuming that there is adequate likeness to facilitate actual understanding.

That is, the Bible does not share the scepticism of the ancient philosophers or the modern philosophers of language concerning "god-talk." That is, from Plato to 21st-century philosophy, the ability for humans to speak about God has been called into question. God is very rarely an object of human experience, and when he is, he seems to reveal himself in very human ways (e.g. Genesis 19), which the classic theologians called "accommodation." So we never experience God "as he is in himself." If human language is fundamentally rooted in our experience, how can we adequately speak of a God who is beyond our experience or, in the philosophers' terms, whose essence is hidden from us? If there is truly a division between the Creator and creature, how can our language be adequate to speak of him? However, the Bible simply assumes that our language is thus competent. God reveals himself throughout the Bible in human words and human ways, and though we are continually reminded that there is a great difference between us and God, we are never led to believe that this chasm inhibits our knowledge of God. God repeatedly acts so that "they may know I am Yahweh," and this self-revelation is accomplished (E.g. Ezek 5:13, 11:10, etc., cf. Exod 14:4). This is not true at the expense of God's transcendence, his genuine difference from and authority over us, but through the wisdom of his creating work. God created humanity like himself and the world in such a way that we can adequately understand God through our understanding of the world. Thus, the likeness God has established between aspects of the created order and between himself and the created order gives unity, the foundation for rationality.

C. The Unity of Conceptual Relations

And the LORD appeared to him by the oaks of Mamre, as he sat at the door of his tent in the heat of the day. He lifted up his eyes and looked, and behold, three men were standing in front of him. – Gen 18:1-2

The unity of Law and likeness gives a foundation for the last form of unity that upholds rationality amidst the flux of particularity, namely, concepts. The Greek philosopher rightly recognized that we use universal or *abstract* language all the time. However, with few exceptions, I will argue that they misunderstand *abstraction*. For the Greeks, the abstract was more real than the concrete, "treeness" was more real (or at least more epistemologically important) than "this Arbutus tree." They thought that reality represented by an abstract term (a universal reality, such as the Forms) was the most significant object of knowledge. There were several exceptions to this (such as several early Stoics who understood the abstract along the same lines we will develop), but this was true for the most part.

The problem is not abstract terms themselves; we use universal or abstract terms every day. Every time we identify that dog as a pug or that oak as a tree, we are involved in some level of abstract thought. However, I contend that a correct understanding of abstract thought does not identify "abstracts" as real things or as important objects of knowledge. Instead, abstracts or universals are "concepts," mental acts and related linguistic signs that facilitate our knowledge of particular things. We will explore this first by revisiting the function of abstraction in the philosophical tradition before turning to a conceptualist account.

a. Abstraction and the Greek Universals

Abstraction properly conceived is a necessary tool in coming to true knowledge of God and his created world. If we want to think intelligently in this world, we need to use abstract thought. Yet if we want to think faithfully, we must think abstractly in the biblical sense, not in the sense of the classic philosophical tradition.

i. Abstract Vs Concrete Thinking

For many philosophers, abstract thinking is set in opposition to concrete thinking. Concrete thought is concerned with the particular objects of our experience. It is not interested in knowing what "dogs" are like; it wants to know what Fido is like. Instead of studying anthropology, concrete thought wants to know about John, an individual human.

Abstract thought, in contrast, is concerned with general categories that encompass particular objects. Abstraction is a generalization (e.g. "Humanity") of related particular objects (e.g. Bill, Bob, Jane, Judy, etc.). Fido is only of interest to the abstract thinker in as much as he sheds light on "dogs." John is only important in as much as he reveals something about "humanity." For the early Greek Philosophers, abstract knowledge was the only thing that truly qualified as knowledge. For Plato and Aristotle, Fido or the oak tree out your front door do not matter. They are not the most important objects of knowledge. True knowledge is of "dogness" (that essential element that defines a dog) or "treeness." In this sense of abstract thought, the differentiating features of particular objects or persons (size, height, colour, pattern, behaviour, personality, history) are not objects of knowledge. Instead, abstract thought focuses on the unity of objects; true knowledge concerns the essence of a human being, a dog, or a tree. To truly know something is to know the essence, that without which it ceases to be (i.e. the definition and accompanying set of properties make something what it is and the absence of which disqualifies a person from being human or a dog from being a dog, for example).

ii. Abstraction and the Possibility of Knowledge

Why in the world, you may be asking yourself, would someone define knowledge in this way? Abstraction in this non-Christian sense, if possible, allows humanity to have autonomous knowledge of everything. That is, if knowledge is found in abstracting the irreducible essence of things, it follows that you will eventually arrive at something true for everything. However, if knowledge is of particular objects, we are doomed to know almost nothing— or at least this would be the result within the systems of the philosophers.

iii. The Result of Non-Christian Abstraction

Therefore, if you want to know anything apart from revelation—if you want to reason autonomously—you must maintain the priority of abstract thought. You must believe that you can know everything without knowing every particular thing. "It certainly seemed," for the Greeks, "that abstraction was the royal road to knowledge, even knowledge of concrete realities."[2] But once we have followed abstract thought to its end—abstract knowledge of everything—what is the knowledge that we have obtained?

What, we may ask, unifies "dogs" and "man?" They are both "animals" in opposition to plants and insects. But plants, insects and animals have in

---

[2] John M. Frame, *The Doctrine of the Knowledge of God*, A Theology of Lordship (Phillipsburg: P&R Publishing, 1987), 173.

common "life." They are all living things. These have in common with certain materials an "organic" nature, so they are all organic things. With inorganic things, they are all potential objects of our experience. Like our own thoughts, objects of experience can be predicated with the attribute "existence." In this way, some philosophers say we have arrived at that category that describes all things, "being." If we know "being," we know everything.

Yet what is our knowledge of this "being?" If it is the bare unity that describes my ideas, rocks, gases, stars, planets, lizards, amoebae, and humans, what do we really know about it? If your thought of "being" contains any "beings" (a rock, element, idea, person, etc.), you are not thinking abstractly enough! Our knowledge of being cannot be of any being and cannot have any descriptive characteristics (colour, height, width, location, etc.). It is, essentially, nothing. As the philosopher Hegel once observed, we cannot distinguish being from non-being! Our ultimate abstract knowledge of everything is the knowledge of nothing. Regarding humanness, the abstraction of humans is nothing like any human, for it is absent of colour, facial patterns, size, etc.; it is absent of anything by which we differ and by which we regularly identify persons as like us. In this way, abstract knowledge yields absolutely no knowledge at all. In the chapter above, we have already raised problems with this view of abstraction and explained much of what the theory was introduced to explain. However, more problems abound.

Related to the above, imagine a "human" without particular features or a definition of "humanness." In the former case, it is impossible; in the latter, a definition adequate to capture our similarities simultaneously fails to tell us anything valuable about us, humans. Or consider the problems caused by language. For Plato and Aristotle, the abstracts or universals corresponded to language (at least in its positive uses, "righteousness" but not "sin," "cleanliness" but not "dirty"; "sin" and "dirty" are thought to be the negation or the contrary of the positive). "Accidental" terms, those that inhere in a subject and are not found apart from one (such as colour, place, size, etc.), were thought to refer to actual properties inhering in a thing. Aristotle rejected the existence of abstracts apart from things, so concepts corresponded to actual properties but only as they are found in things. However, Plato believed that the abstracts existed above things, that is, that they were more real than them and caused them to be the way they are (to be red is to participate in Redness). Nominal or "substantial" terms likewise referred to real things, horses, humans, etc. This belief led to a series of issues in Plato's theory and also for Aristotle, though the problems faced by Aristotle were different than those faced by Plato.[3] The problem with such thinking, that terms correspond exactly to reality, is that it does not work within a single language, let alone across multiple languages. Consider the English term "table"; it shares considerable overlap but is undoubtedly not identical with the Greek term τράπεζα (**trapeza**) and the Hebrew שׁוּלְחָן (šûlḥān). There is no one abstract concept that corresponds to each of these terms.

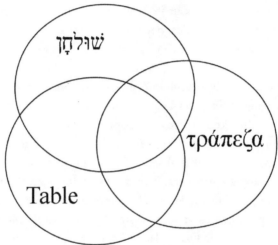

Overlapping Fields of Reference

Or consider the Hebrew word דָּג (dāg), translated "fish": it overlaps considerably with the English term "fish," yet refers to several things that would probably not be called a "fish" today (Jonah's "fish" for example). Consider the English term "love," which is used to translate the separate Greek words φιλέω (**phileō**), ἀγαπάω (**agapaō**), ἐράω (**eraō**), and στέργω (**stergō**). Some of these may be better translated with other English words, but they all overlap at some point with the everyday use of the term "love." Such a list could go on indefinitely: the point is, each word seems to refer to

---

[3] See Plato's *Parmenides*, especially the final section, and Aristotle's *Categories*. Problems or *aporia* with Aristotle's view are found throughout his works, especially *Physics, Generation and Corruption,* and *Metaphysics.*

a different totality of things, so we could say that each word has a different concept (though doing so makes things even more complicated!). There is surely not an abstract entity for each of these terms—**šûlḥan-ness**, tableness, trapeza-ness, etc. Yet they overlap significantly: what they have in common is their shared referents. The phenomena of linguistic diversity, such that different languages divide the world up in different ways (in one language, there might be less than ten words for colours, in another, upwards of 50), indicates that words do not correspond directly to reality (such that every word has a "right" meaning) and that they divide the experienced world in different but mutually compatible ways.[4] Not only is linguistic diversity a problem for the view that language connects directly to abstract, extra-mental realities, but there is also a significant body of evidence that animals have concepts, though they lack the advanced language skills of humans. This suggests that concepts precede language and are initially independent of it. However, the use of language creates and refines concepts, leading to the conclusions that concepts are mental equipment, as is language, but that the two have some measure of independent operation.[5] The problem with the philosopher's view of abstraction is that it is not evidently the way our minds work, nor how language works, nor a necessary implication of the world's structure, as we saw in the previous chapters.

---

[4] Cf. Vern S. Poythress, *Symphonic Theology: The Validity of Multiple Perspectives in Theology* (Grand Rapids: Academie Books, 1987); Moisés Silva, *Biblical Words and Their Meaning: An Introduction to Lexical Semantics*, rev. and expanded ed. (Grand Rapids: Zondervan, 1994); Vern S. Poythress, *In the Beginning Was the Word: Language: A God-Centered Approach* (Wheaton: Crossway Books, 2009); Nicholas J. Ellis, "Biblical Exegesis and Linguistics: A Prodigal History," in *Linguistics and New Testament Greek: Key Issues in the Current Debate*, ed. David Alan Black and Benjamin L Merkle (Grand Rapids: Baker Publishing Group, 2020).

[5] Different studies work with different definitions of concepts, and there is a significant potential for an alternate interpretation in the tests regarding animals, but I think these points are still consistent with the evidence. Cf. Polanyi, *Personal Knowledge*, chaps. 5, passim; Kathleen Callow, *Man and Message: A Guide to Meaning-Based Text Analysis* (Lanham, Md: Summer Institute of Linguistics, University Press of America, 1998), 53; Thomas R. Zentall et al., "Concept Learning in Animals," *Comparative Cognition & Behavior Reviews* 3 (2008); Iain McGilchrist, *The Master and His Emissary: The Divided Brain and the Making of the Western World*, New expanded edition. (New Haven: Yale University Press, 2019), passim; Maximilian E. Kirschhock, Helen M. Ditz, and Andreas Nieder, "Behavioral and Neuronal Representation of Numerosity Zero in the Crow," *Journal of Neuroscience* 41, no. 22 (June 2, 2021): 4889–4896.

b. Abstraction from a Different Perspective

However, I think a better account of abstraction can be given, one that coheres well with what we have seen thus far. In the early 14th century, William of Ockham argued against various views of the universals that had been held up until his time. He argued against their metaphysical reality: they did not cause properties or change in extra-mental objects; they were not *real* in any extra-mental sense. However, they did have a role in human thought. He argued that universal concepts, or abstract cognitions, were mental acts that referred to multiple extra-mental objects according to their likeness. That is, James, John, and Peter have real similarities. I cognize each of them as individuals and develop a mental "sign" that refers to all of these individuals. This mental sign or act is not itself a thing, an idea or image, but a mental act that refers to all individuals that are most similar to these three men, that is, to anything that is "human." This linguistic sign itself represents the mental sign or concept. Ockham's view is complicated, but several important observations can be made from Ockham's thought. One the hand, he does not deny the existence of universal terms and concepts, such as "human." "Human" refers to particular individuals because they have something genuinely in common. I can thus use the term "human" in language and logic to communicate something of that commonality. Yet, for Ockham, this concept does not stand apart from the particulars I experience; it merely refers to them. That is, it is not a formula or image that is equally James, John, and Peter—taking away all their differences—but it is merely a placeholder for all such similar entities so that the mind may draw on its previous experience of such things in order to analyse new experience and communicate previous experience. A similar view has been developed and expressed by cognitive linguistics in recent decades. Kathleen Callows argues, "Rather than considering concepts as things, we should consider them habitual events."[6] That is, as we grow, we mentally group objects together, Peter, James, John, or Fido, Rex, and Fluffy. We develop a habit of automatically identifying those things that are similar and grouping them together. A concept is, therefore, not an abstract definition drawn from each of the particulars but is the act of connecting these particulars with one another.

As we speak about "humans," we invoke or refer to a broad experience

---

[6] Callow, *Man and Message*, 53.

of things we have grouped together, often isolating one relation that obtains among them (such as their physical form, abilities, possession of mind, language, etc.). As a term, "human" refers to a concept, which isolates a specific group of things that are alike in certain ways. We could thus describe the abstraction signified by universal terms as a particular relationship between objects. Not all language functions in this way, but this holds for abstract qualities (e.g. colour), verbs and many abstract nouns (e.g. to love, love; to do good, goodness), and categorical nouns (e.g. human, animal, house).

As we will see in the following chapters, a colour is both definable and indefinable. We can identify the cause of our perception of colour so that we could define red as the perception of a certain wavelength of light. But this does not describe "red." "Red" is an experience that we know but cannot explain or define; all we can do is point to red things and identify other red things. "Red" as a colour—a perception—is always a red something. Indeed, we identify it as a specific relationship—a likeness—between many otherwise disparate objects.

Similarly, try as I may, I cannot define "love," either the act or the abstract. I can, however, identify acts of love. Acts that qualify as "love" meet in a rich concept that weaves together a complex set of factors, such as what is done, the motivations for it being done, the circumstances, and the reception of the act: all these are caught up in a kiss being an act of love and not merely a greeting, or in the giving of a gift. Surprisingly, the Bible never defines love in any philosophical sense: when Jesus wants to identify love, he points to his actions and sacrifice (John 13:34, 15:13; cf. 1 John 4:10); John points to God himself (1 John 4:16). However, love is central to the biblical ethic: the two greatest commands are love God and your neighbour as yourself (Mark 12:29-31). Instead of giving an abstract definition, the Bible repeatedly shows us what is not and is loving. In particular, the Bible shows us God's acts towards his people.

Finally, it should be clear how this is true for categorical nouns. The likeness between things varies: for many people, the concept of table revolves around function, namely, what a surface is used for. The concept of "human" changes depending on the context, but usually has the sense of common lineage: central to the biblical concept of humanity is its common descent from Adam. However, in other contexts, the term "human" merely refers to a concept of the human form, so that Yahweh and his angels may be called "men" (e.g. Gen 19).

A mental concept thus refers to the mental act of drawing together particular things according to their likeness. Such concepts are indefinite: there may be a mental concept for every relation that obtains between all particulars *I* experience. Thus, my concepts will differ in some ways from yours. However, God would possess every possible concept that his creatures may develop. As recognized by Ockham, concepts do not exist as mental acts alone; we also communicate concepts using language. All communication is by necessity restrictive: it predicates (i.e. so and so is *something*), drawing our focus on certain features or states of affairs and thus bracketing out others. Universal terms describe relationships we perceive between the particular objects of our experience. To say that "humans have minds" simultaneously restricts the concept "human" to certain things with minds and focuses on that very likeness. If I have never experienced humans before but have a concept of God and spirits as beings with minds ("persons"), the statement "humans have minds" incorporates humans into my previous concept of persons or things with "minds."

The relationships indicated by concepts are not themselves objects of knowledge but conceptual bridges that allow us to utilize the knowledge we already have in understanding new objects we experience. For example, the knowledge of Fido the poodle, Maximus Rex the pug, and Wolf the husky would allow someone to identify specific features and behaviours exhibited by the dog sitting outside the Blenz coffee shop on the corner of Cornwall Avenue and Walnut Street in Vancouver, Canada. So, concepts serve a rational function in our intellect. In a rich enough context, universal terms allow us to communicate new concepts to others. If I have never previously experienced a monkey, I may develop a concept of a monkey from certain animals at the zoo; by learning the term "monkey," I may then expand my knowledge of these animals by reading about other particulars in videos, images, and texts. My concept of a "monkey" will be different from yours, but will overlap in a significant way and so facilitate communication. However, in every case, concepts ultimately resolve into particulars. Because mental and communicative concepts refer to particulars, they are always to some extent concrete, not purely abstract. "Monkey" refers to certain objects according to what they have in common, so it indicates a specific likeness between them and indicates certain features held by these objects (such as prehensile tail). Yet no definition will suffice to capture the rich variety that is found across the many objects of a concept: though monkeys are all different in colour, the concept of monkey is not colourless. Such a variety of experiences juxtaposed with likeness cannot be captured in an abstract definition (which excises all differences in search of unity) but is upheld by our mental concepts. In sum, mental concepts are habitual events grouping objects, and communicative acts signify such events, often isolating particular relationships between objects.

i. An Abstraction is a Particular Relationship Between Objects

I have defined a concept as a mental act or "habitual event" of relating particulars; terms refer to concepts, presenting a particular relationship between objects with language. I think this is a definition of abstraction consistent with our experience as interpreted by the Bible. That we can talk about "humanity," "existence," "smallness," "largeness," etc. demonstrates that we use abstract thought.

Revisiting abstract nouns, I know that I have no definition of "love" or "goodness." But neither do I have a single exemplar of love in mind, an isolated event with no relation.[7] Instead, our concepts of love refer to a series of events that we deem exemplary of "love." If love is neither a floating abstract definition that lays behind these events nor a random assortment of events, what remains is that "love" is a relationship between these events. Love describes a particular feature of these events that is drawn out when they are viewed in relationship with one another. It is not a "part" of these events, as if you could take an instance of me saying "I love you" to Nicole and dissect it into parts—it is part speech, love, communication, respect, etc. Instead, love describes one way of looking at this event as it shares commonality with other similar events; it is a perspective by which all these events can be viewed.

---

[7] Withing cognitive linguistics, it is often supposed that concepts have a "prototype," or an exemplar to which other objects are related. I am not convinced that the data supports this theory nor that it has as much explanatory power as the view articulated above.

c. Problems with This View

I believe that such a definition of abstraction, as a particular relationship between objects (whether things or events) makes sense of what goes on with abstract thought. For our purposes, three problems emerge as concerns for this view. First, such a definition of love runs the risk of destroying communication: how do I know my perception of the relationship I call "love" is the same as yours? If there is no abstract definition of love by which we can compare our selection of examples of love, how do we know who is "right" or even that we agree? This then raises two more problems. Morality assumes that there is some standard by which we can determine which actions, thoughts, or attitudes are genuine examples of "love"; is that undermined by this definition? If morality is not undermined, how do humans access this standard—however it is now defined?

i. Problem One

First, there is indeed a sense in which all our abstract terms are subjective and arbitrary—yet this need not destroy the possibility of communication. That language is arbitrary and subjective is evident with a bit of thought: the symbol "d-o-g" is no more fitting for a dog than the symbol "c-a-t." In this sense, language is arbitrary. The fact that the definition of "love" among Christians differs from that of Atheists and that the very word "love" differs from the related words in other languages (e.g. ἔρως, ἀγάπη, φιλέω, אהב, quiero, amo, adoro) shows that "love" itself is a subjective term. But this does not necessarily destroy communication or morality. To the contrary, if we notice that the Spanish word quiero at times means "I love you" but can mean something more sexual, we do not say that "quiero" is being used wrongly because it does not equal our understanding of "love." Instead, we listen and learn the range of meanings quiero has. The point is this, everyone uses the word "love" or the equivalent in other languages to mean different things; to learn what someone else means by "love," we pay attention to how they use it. We identify the relationship that holds among all these uses, the similarities they all have. So, the subjectivity of our definition of abstraction does not destroy communication; to the contrary, it fits very well with how we learn a language and technical terms (i.e. particularly refined abstract terms). An implication of this is that humans must intentionally understand how others are using language to make communication possible. This means that communication is a moral act, one for which God will hold us accountable.[8]

ii. Problem Two

Our answer leads us to the second problem: for behaviour to be moral (judged good or bad), it must be measured by a standard that cannot be relative to each person. My definition of abstraction so far seems to endanger this, for it is usual to understand the moral standards as objective, abstract concepts. However, this is not a necessary conclusion. As we have seen, abstraction is a personal concept, the perception of relationships between objects. Therefore, an impersonal standard is out of the question. However, God—the true measure of right and wrong—is not an impersonal standard. We can define the standards of morality (moral goodness, love, truth, kindness, etc.) as God's perception of particular relationships between events (broadly defined to include actions, thoughts, feelings, etc.). "Love" as it matters for declaring something morally right or wrong is not my definition of love, nor the Greek definition of ἀγάπη (*agapē*, "love"), but God's definition of love. Our answer here brings us to the last problem.

iii. Problem Three

If the standard for truth and morality is God's interpretation of events, how do we have access to God's standards? We need to answer this in two ways, for we need to explain both the explicit standards for judging behaviour and the implicit "work of the law" that is imprinted on human hearts (cf. Rom 2:12-16). To explain the knowledge all human beings have of God's expectations, ultimately that they worship and obey him (Rom 2:18-32), we must appeal to something like innate ideas. As David Hume long ago showed, it is impossible to derive an "ought" statement from an "is": we cannot determine what we ought to think and do from our experience alone, so we need something by which to interpret our experience and declare it good or bad. Such a "something" cannot come from experience (a bare "is").[9]

---

[8] Cf. *The Gift of Knowing*, God's Gifts for the Christian Life – Part 1 Vol. 1 (Vancouver, Teleioteti 2019).

[9] If every "is" implies an ought, then the reality of murder, assault, etc. would indicate the appropriateness or even the necessity of such things. If one were to discriminate and say that certain realities, such as what is "natural" as opposed to human-made, are morally normative, the problem remains. On the one hand, assault

However, the Bible makes it clear that those without special revelation know what they ought to do: they recognize certain acts as wrong and others as right (e.g. Rom 1:18-3:). Humans must, therefore, have the innate ability to identify moral acts, meaning they have the ability to develop moral concepts. In *The Gift of Knowing*, I suggested that this innateness may be explained as a sort of template: our minds are hardwired to identify certain features of the world and give them an appropriate evaluation, thus making these a normative concept. I still find this explanation necessary; I think our minds do have something like templates for building concepts of colours and things (giving unity to the cacophony of sensation we are confronted with; see Part 3). However, since writing *The Gift of Knowing*, I have developed my thinking on moral concepts. We have seen already that God himself is the standard of morality: his deeds and evaluations become the norms for our deeds and evaluations. At the heart of Romans 1-2, where Paul clearly asserts the universal knowledge of God's law, Paul first claims that all humans know God.[10] Therefore, it seems the claim that all humans know God's law is an implication of all people knowing God's "invisible attributes, namely, his eternal power and divine nature" (Rom 1:20a). If we know God, we will have some sense of how he will evaluate reality, including our actions and the actions of others. However, this adds another dimension to our problem: what do we do with this knowledge? Most people would not confess to knowing God in this way.

Our argument so far has opened space for a solution. By developing concepts in terms of mental acts and the fundamental objects of knowledge as particulars, we have broadened the concept of knowledge beyond propositions and explicit beliefs. The knowledge of persons, for example, cannot be reduced to propositions: it includes them but cannot be reduced to them.[11] I know Nicole, my wife, better than anyone else does (or so I

---

and killing are still normative (as they are present throughout the natural world); on the other, the principle used to differentiate between what realities are normative (natural vs. human-made) is arbitrary and needs justification. Thus, moral judgment requires a moral standard or principle by which the situation in question can be judged.

[10] Here, I discuss the function of the knowledge of God in conscious. We will look at this passage further below.

[11] Cf. Frame, *The Doctrine of the Knowledge*, 44–48.

would claim), yet her mom and sisters likely have more factual knowledge about Nicole's life than I do. Knowledge of persons is complex, involving knowledge of their past and present with the result that we can anticipate their future, namely, how they will respond and what they may desire. Such knowledge facilitates communication, empathy, and relationships in general. This sort of knowledge (the knowledge of persons) is attendant in all my interactions with Nicole but is always tacit, part of the interpretive framework by which I interpret and construct the world around me.[12] If the knowledge of God possessed by all humans is propositional knowledge, we run into a problem: few people would consciously acknowledge this knowledge. However, if the knowledge of God we all possess is tacit, it may or may not correspond to conscious belief.

For someone who professes faith in the God of the Bible, this knowledge is analogous to the knowledge I have of my wife, Nicole: it is active in all my interpretive endeavours and is complemented by explicit association with Yahweh and propositional knowledge of his character and works (e.g. he is righteous, covenanted with his people, became incarnate, rules all things, etc.). However, for those without this conscious belief, the knowledge of Yahweh will still shape their interaction with his world: they will not consciously connect their perception of order and consistency in nature with God's faithfulness, but they will nevertheless interpret the world in light of this truth. Indeed, as Paul goes on to write, they may associate what they know of God—his "invisible attributes, namely, eternal power and divine nature" (Rom 1:20a)—with elements of the created order, deifying things that are not God, whether spiritual or human persons or even nature itself (Rom 1:21-25). As it concerns the innate sense of morality Paul identifies in these early chapters of Romans (often call conscience), person-knowledge of God (as described above on analogy with our knowledge of human persons) explains how we may innately know God's moral will concerning what we ought to and ought not to do (Rom 1:21, 32; 2:14-15). If, as I have argued, morality is rooted in God's nature reflected in verbal revelation and in his deeds, then knowing God enables us to anticipate what he approves of and disapproves of—as knowing Nicole allows me to anticipate what would please or displease her.

---

[12] See further, *The Gift of Knowing;* Polanyi, *Personal Knowledge*, 49–68, 69–195; Michael Polanyi, *The Tacit Dimension* (Chicago; London: University of Chicago Press, 2009).

So, God has given all human beings the ability from birth to correlate specific experiences with his standards, judging them to be right or wrong. Whether we call an act ἀγαπή or love, we can judge it to be right or wrong. Yet this innate judge, our conscience, is not perfect: we twist and ignore it, leaving it marred (Rom 1:18-3:20). Therefore, we need an explicit revelation of God's moral standard by which we can correct our sinful distortions and be intentional in pursuing obedience to God.

I intend, of course, the Bible. If we learn what other people mean by "love" by studying what they identify as "love," we learn what God means by "love" by studying those things he identifies. Looking at Scripture, we are taught that God is love. We are taught that love is an essential way to understand who God is and that only by understanding who God is will we understand love (1 John 4:7-12). Everything we identify as "love" is only such, therefore, because it reflects this aspect of God's character. Love is a perspective by which we can view God's actions within his triune-self (e.g. John 17) and towards his creation. By looking at this pattern of God's activity, we can then identify what thoughts, actions, attitudes, etc. are loving or not. This pattern is sometimes described (1 Corinthians 13) and sometimes narrated (Exodus) but it is this, the character of God displayed through his actions (including word and deed) and revealed to us in Scripture that gives us a standard for what is and is not love. Therefore, the concept of "love," as our example for right loving, is a particular relationship that we identify between acts that are consistent with what God has shown us about his loving character. Thus, we have two ways to access God's perfect standard. First, all humans have person-knowledge of God, by which we intuitively identify right and wrong. However, this knowledge is marred by sin; we often need correction. Second, we have the revelation of God's character and his interpretation of many events and actions throughout history. This revelation corrects our knowledge of God and our evaluations of truth and goodness.

Before concluding, we can also observe how our argument explains how human language is adequate for speaking of God. That is, given that God is transcendent—utterly beyond us—and outside of our experience, how do our concepts, developed it would seem from our experience, allow us to speak and think rightly of him? Would not thoughts of the created order have to bring God down to the level of that order to speak rightly of him?

In response, we saw that God has structured the world to reflect his own faithfulness and has given us minds competent to discern consistency in the world. Given that we interpret the world with the presupposition of God's faithfulness (i.e. stability or consistency), our interpretation of the world as stable and consistent moves from God as he has made himself known to the world, not from the world to God. Furthermore, he has created humanity and the world with the adequate likeness that it might be an effective revelation of his character, as is evident throughout Scripture. This is clear both in its statements and the assumption that our language is adequate to speak of him. Finally, we are able to interpret actions and events as good or bad, right or wrong, loving or unloving *because* God has made himself personally known in our interpretive hardware: he has wired humanity with person-knowledge of himself. Thus, our concepts do not move from earthly analogies to God but from God to earthly things. If God is eternally triune, then it would not be preposterous to suppose that the person-knowledge of God contains knowledge of his triune-self, including his eternal fatherhood. Thus, we can discern a good father from a bad father because we know God who is the perfect father: our understanding of earthly fathers does not first inform our knowledge of God as father, but our knowledge of God informs our evaluation of earthly fatherhood. Of course, the impact of earthly fathers often does affect our interpretation of God as Father (cf. Rom 2:15), so we need Scripture to perfect our innate but distorted knowledge.

D. Conclusion

In this chapter, I have argued that the priority of the particular indicated by the Bible does not destroy reason or rationality, though it certainly limits it. We can interpret the world, have true and certain knowledge, and anticipate the regularity of our experience because God has carefully crafted his creation as the perfect medium of his self-revelation and for his creatures' creative obedience (i.e. ruling the earth as his representatives). His word upholds the consistent functioning of the world; the created world was created to be like God and like to itself so that humans could know God and his world; finally, the human mind was created with the ability to draw relations between things in order to better understand each thing in light of similar things. Ultimately, regularity, likeness, and conceptuality enable us to know God. We know God as Father because he has made earthly fathers like him; we know God as powerful because we encounter power in this world and his Word; etc. The biblical worldview upholds unity and plurality in a way the Greeks did not envision: the particular is primary, yet the particular is always mentally interpreted in relation to other things. This element of "interpretation" is ambiguous thus far: it will be the object of Part 3 to outline the significant ways in which the mind is involved in interpreting the world and the relationship between this interpretation, truth, and communication. It is fitting for us to respond to the beauty and wisdom of God's creation, so perfect for facilitating human understanding, as Paul once responded to God's wisdom in salvation:

> Oh, the depth of the riches and wisdom and knowledge of God! How unsearchable are his judgments and how inscrutable his ways!
>
> "For who has known the mind of the Lord,
>   or who has been his counselor?"
> "Or who has given a gift to him
>   that he might be repaid?"
>
> For from him and through him and to him are all things. To him be glory forever. Amen. (Romans 11:33-36)

—PART 3—

The Problem of the External World

7

THE END OF EMPIRICISM

A. Modernism – The World of the Senses

To say that "Modernism" is the "world of the senses" is not to say that all modern philosophy was supremely concerned with the sensible world. There were also idealists and rationalists who focused on the mind in one way or another, yet the overall concern of this time was to justify the scientific discipline.[1] The rationalists were concerned with building a foundation of certain knowledge from which other disciplines such as science could be performed; the empiricists attempted to probe the extent of what could be known through senses alone. The former school of philosophy, the rationalists, is primarily associated with Continental Europe; the latter school, the empiricists, with Britain.

The father of Modern philosophy is often thought to be Rene Descartes (1596-1650). Descartes considered himself a faithful Catholic. However, like the atheistic philosophers before him, Descartes starting point for philosophy is the self—the one thing of which he thought we could be most

---

[1] Idealism refers to a metaphysical view that reality is ultimately mental. That is, either what we perceive as physical is actually immaterial mental content or all we can know is our mental perception. Rationalism gives priority to the mind over the senses in attaining knowledge. Many rationalists would say that the senses yield no true knowledge.

certain. Though Descartes is important in many respects, the British Empiricists are more important for our purposes.

a. *George Berkeley*

According to Immanuel Kant (one of the most influential philosophers in recent history), it was the British philosopher David Hume who "awoke" him from his "dogmatic slumber," from his philosophical rationalism. However, it was George Berkeley who developed many of the radical ideas that Hume would employ in pursuit of an atheistic agenda.

George Berkeley was an Anglican bishop in Ireland during the 17th century. He adopted a view of human knowledge much like that of William of Ockham, within which all human knowledge pertained to particular things. Berkeley went farther than Ockham by arguing that not only the universal but also the particular could be explained as mental activity. Instead of positing an extramental substance that could cause all our sense experience, such as a tree that caused our sense of rough, brown bark and green leaves, he argued that all experience could be explained by the direct activity of God, who was the cause of the various experiences we have. Berkely intended to rule out atheism and scepticism, but David Hume developed similar arguments in the opposite direction, toward scepticism.

b. *David Hume*

The most influential British Empiricist was, perhaps, David Hume (1711-1776). David Hume was ferociously consistent in his philosophy, to the extent that almost all knowledge was cast into doubt. Hume was no friend of Christianity, yet his writing shows just how hopeless is a philosophy built on reason alone.

As for ontology, Hume is most important in showing how hopeless the rational investigation of the connection between our mind and the outside world can become. For Hume, *analytic truths* can be known by the meaning of the words themselves, such as statements about mathematics and logic, but all other knowledge must be tested by the senses. Knowledge in the latter sense can be classified as impressions and ideas. Impressions are immediate sensory data. Ideas are mental concepts of objects derived from impressions, such as the concepts of that table or this house as found in our memory. For Hume, ideas are not 100% reliable and thus must be traced back to the impressions that created them for verification.

The assumption that all non-analytic truths (i.e. all truths that are not self-evident) must be tested by the senses rules out much of the ontological speculation of Hume's predecessors. Any search for a unifying "substance," such as a basic matter shared by all things, is impossible: we neither have nor can have experience of such a thing. Not only is it impossible to find an abstract concept that gives knowledge of everything, even the laws necessary to interpret the world have no basis in the senses. If we only sense diversity, we have no reason to believe that there is ultimate unity. Whereas Berkeley wanted to prevent scepticism by positing that God stood behind all human experience, thus making that experience consistent and trustworthy, Hume argued that we must be sceptical about the very existence of God.

If it is only reasonable to believe something demonstrated by the senses, the supernatural realm is ruled out as unreasonable. Hume did not make any metaphysical claim that God and miracles do not exist or cannot happen. He only claimed that there is no reasonable way to know that a miracle occurred or that God exists. We have no sense experience of God, so if someone tells us that God exists, how can we verify this claim? The same is true for miracles. Miracles are, by definition, rare events. As such, we will not have previous sense experiences of them. If we have never experienced a resurrection, it is only reasonable to doubt the idea of a resurrection. It is more reasonable to assume that any experience of a miracle is a false idea than to believe it without sense verification:

> Hume argues that there can never be sufficient evidence to affirm that a miracle has taken place. He begins by defining *miracle* as a violation of a law of nature. But that definition makes it impossible for us to believe that any event was a miracle. We always have more evidence, says Hume, for the normal course of nature than we have for any claimed exception to it. So when confronted with a strange event, we should always prefer natural explanations of it to supernatural explanations. Says Hume, it is always more likely that the witnesses misunderstood or misrepresented the event than that it was a violation of the laws of nature.[2]

By demanding a strict empirical standard for truth, Hume rules out many facets of ontology in general. In particular, he places God and the search for

[2] Frame, *A History*, 202.

unity amidst the plurality of experience beyond the bounds of reason. If ontology seeks to explain knowledge and its relation both to experience and truth, to our minds and the external world, Hume's scepticism rules it out. We have no access to the outside world nor to a God who would reveal anything about it. Furthermore, we have no access to a standard above ourselves to claim anything like transcendent truth (i.e. truth that is always valid for all people). The laws that appear to regulate our experience are reduced to psychology, and supernatural claims are purely claims of faith, not reason:[3]

> If we take in our hand any volume; of divinity or school metaphysics, for instance; let us ask, Does it contain any abstract reasoning concerning quantity or number [i.e., analytic truth]? No. Does it contain any experimental reasoning concerning matter of fact and existence [i.e., empirical truth]? No. Commit it then to the flames: for it can contain nothing but sophistry and illusion.[4]

c. Immanuel Kant

Before Immanuel Kant (1724-1804), philosophy evolved along different trajectories in continental Europe and Britain. The German thinker Kant changed this by bringing together the rationalism of the continent with the empiricism of Britain.

Where does one go after the scepticism of Hume? How could philosophy be pursued if everything must be subject to the test of experience? Kant's answer was something called the transcendental method. He reasoned not by deducing philosophical truths from several basic premises, as Descartes and the rationalists did, nor by deriving truth from sense experience. He argued instead from what must necessarily be so if knowledge is possible. That is, assuming that one can have knowledge, he asked, what must the world be

---

[3] This may sound like a twisted way of protecting Christian belief from science and philosophy, in a way similar to later protestant philosophers. However, Hume appears to be much more aggressively atheistic; though Christian belief is not proved wrong, it is shown to be utterly unreasonable. The conclusion of his *Dialogues Concerning Natural Religion* suggests that his goal is to show that after reason is done with it, Christianity is essentially meaningless.

[4] This is from Hume's *An Enquiry concerning Human Understanding*, 12.3.

like?[5] What are the conditions that make knowledge possible? His answer was a two-world schema: there is the *noumenal* world and the *phenomenal* world.

The noumenal world is the world of what is, the actual. The phenomenal world is the world of the mind, of experience. We do not know anything about the noumenal world; our mind defines everything we experience. Our senses receive from the noumenal world something which Kant called *percepts,* bare "experience." *Percepts* have no content; our mind receives the percept and defines it with qualities such as treeness, brown, leafness, green, 8 feet tall, etc. There is something out there, but everything we know about the tree is imposed by our minds on the *percept* received. Therefore, we cannot know anything about reality; we can only know about our own mind. Nevertheless, the phenomenal world is the realm where science is safe to function apart from the criticism of philosophy. Now, someone may ask how we can even know that the noumenal exists if all our experience is mental. For Kant, the noumenal world must exist to explain our experience. Similarly, "god" must exist to explain ethics.

Thus, there is an external world in Kant's philosophy, but we cannot know anything about it. There is also a god, yet we cannot know anything about it. God exists merely as the goal of ethics; god is essentially the idea that appropriate ethical behaviour will be rewarded, justifying the effort to be virtuous. Kant was insistent that morality could not be done with any motive of self-benefit, yet for morality to make sense at all, there must be the promise that in the hereafter, good will be rewarded and evil punished. God is the necessary principle to this effect. We cannot know that this god exists, nor that the world exists, but we must nevertheless live "as if" they exist, for only in this way is a reasonable and ethical life possible.

With Kant we observe a significant shift. For Plato, the stable reality that made knowledge possible was the external world of the Forms. Kant

---

[5] In the *Critique of Pure Reason,* Kant defines a certain form of knowledge he called "synthetic *a priori*" propositions, that is, truths which do not depend on sense experience and yet are not analytic. An analytic proposition such as "all bachelors are married" is self-evidently true, for the predicate ("married") is part of the subject ("bachelor"). A synthetic proposition, on the other hand, is one where the predicate is related to the subject but is not implied in it ("all bodies are heavy," that is, affected by gravity). The book then investigates whether synthetic a priori propositions are possible and how they can be so.

essentially reverses this: the stability necessary is imposed on the unknowable world by our minds. The forms do not exist beyond our minds but are an essential feature of our cognitive faculties. For Kant, ontology is absorbed into the thinking subject: it is all about the mind and what it must believe if reason is to be accepted. For Kant, the nature of reality is out of humanity's reach.

Kant and Hume leave us in an uncomfortable place regarding metaphysics; in different ways, they both argue that metaphysics is impossible. Their influence is still felt in modern philosophy, especially in certain forms of 20th-century liberal theology and in the Postmodern rejection of metaphysics. For ontology, Kant's position is similar to early Hellenistic philosophy in several ways. The extra-mental world is ultimately one, undifferentiated and unknowable; it is pure potentiality. The mind is the sole source of stability and form, giving shape to the potentiality of the world. The question of "universals" has faded from view, but if they exist, they are an imposition of our mind on the noumenal world. As with Berkeley, all qualities, such as location, colour, and all form (the similarity Plato and Aristotle identified as essence) are qualities of the mind, not of an external subject. It would thus seem that truth itself is lost, but this is not the position that Kant took. For Kant, the mental framework by which the noumenal world was interpreted was not individual but collective, the shared framework of humanity. However, there seems to be no compelling reason to accept this as the case. Furthermore, apart from revelation, Berkeley's claim that God upholds the unity of experience across all minds is similarly untenable.

B. Conclusion

Philosophy did not stop with Kant. Indeed, it has developed at a mind-boggling pace ever since. Space does not allow us to explore the developments leading up to our time. However, what we have seen thus far has set the tone for the contemporary discussion, at least as far as ontology is concerned. The conclusion of Berkeley, Hume, and Kant concerning the mind's power to form the world around us is widely acknowledged. The atheism of Kant and Hume is generally accepted, so positions within which God has a crucial function are not commonplace. The problem of the universal remains contentious, as does the nature of truth. However, in the work of Kant, Berkeley's claim that reality is mentally constructed was solidified and has become the basis for much contemporary philosophical discussion, both Christian and non-Christian.

Further Reading

George Berkeley, *Principles of Human Knowledge* [A]
George Berkeley, *Three Dialogues* [A][6]
Joshua R. Farris, S. Mark Hamilton, and James S. Spiegel, *Idealism and Christian Theology: Idealism and Christianity Volume 1* [A]
John Frame, *A History of Western Philosophy and Theology* [B-I]
David Hume, *Dialogues Concerning Natural Religion* [A]
David Hume, *An Enquiry into the Human Understanding* [A][7]
Michael Polanyi, *Personal Knowledge: Towards a Post-Critical Philosophy* [A]
Michael Polanyi, *The Tacit Dimension* [I][8]

---

[6] *Principles* is a highly abstract work. Berkeley wrote the *Three Dialogues* to present his main argument for subjective idealism in a more accessible and persuasive manner.

[7] The *Dialogues* argues against the possibility of natural religion; having dismissed the possibility of revelation elsewhere, the dialogue presumes that the question of God's existence is meaningless. In the end, we can have no answer and it makes no difference. *The Enquiry* summarises the main argument of Hume's larger *A Treatise on Human Nature* but is still a difficult work for those without a philosophical background.

[8] In *Personal Knowledge* and *The Tacit Dimension*, Polanyi agrees that objective knowledge is impossible, our minds are actively involved in presenting us the world we perceive in experience. However, this does not mean we cannot have truth or know the world outside of us. *Personal Knowledge* has many profound insights but settles on a decidedly unconvincing account of truth as personal assent. *The Tacit Dimension* presents many of what I would judge to be the most important theses in *Personal Knowledge* in an easier manner.

8

INTERPRETATION: BRING THE
WORLD INTO BEING

And God said, "Let there be light," and there was light.
And God saw that the light was good. And God separated
the light from the darkness. God called the light Day, and
the darkness he called Night. And there was evening and
there was morning, the first day. – Genesis 1:3-5

The natural person does not accept the things of the Spirit
of God, for they are folly to him, and he is not able to
understand them because they are spiritually discerned.
The spiritual person judges all things, but is himself to be
judged by no one. "For who has understood the mind of
the Lord so as to instruct him?" But we have the mind of
Christ. – 1 Corinthians 2:14-16

How often have you thought of the mind's activity in presenting the world
to you? For many Greek philosophers, the world of the senses was
untrustworthy because it was always changing, and our minds were
susceptible to illusion. However, the basic reality of the extra-mental world
was not in question: there was a world out there constructed in a certain way,
accessible to reason. With the rise of the empirical sciences in the mid-2nd
millennium, it quickly became apparent that nature was not objectively

presented to the human mind. Within philosophy, this was already being introduced in the 14th century with William of Ockham; it would be developed extensively by the British Empiricists and Immanuel Kant. In the world of the physical sciences, the subjectivity of the world was recognized by some, such as the philosophers Michael Polanyi and Thomas Kuhn, and ignored by many others, such as Richard Dawkins.

At some point, perhaps in high school, you probably heard the question, "If a tree falls in a forest with no one to hear it, does it make a sound?" At first this sounds sophistical (i.e. pointlessly sceptical), but it raises an important issue. Our reflexive response would be, "of course it does!" But, if we exclude for the moment the presence of God (whose existence means that there is always someone "hearing"), such an answer confuses the meaning of the term "sound." That is, if we acknowledge that a tree has indeed fallen, then it will, of course, create vibrations through the air. However, vibrations in the air *are not sound*; they are merely the cause of sound. That is, sound is *an interpretation* of vibrations, a mental construal as to their significance. Our ears receive the vibrations caused by the tree's fall and present them to us as the experience of sound. However, a deaf person will be acted on by the vibrations and yet not have the same experience, for their physical faculties did not present the sense data to their mental faculties. Someone who has perfectly functioning physical faculties may experience cognitive difficulties interpreting sound with the result that their experience is not the same as the average person. In these ways, "sound," as we usually construe it, does not exist outside of the mind and, therefore, does not exist without an interpreter. The cause of sound is present when the unobserved tree falls, but "sound" is not. Consider colour. Colour is the mental perception of specific wavelengths of light, but our perception of colour depends not only on functioning physical faculties but also corresponding mental faculties. Someone who is colour blind will have a different experience from someone who is not colour blind in response to the same stimuli.

Not only are traditional qualities like colour subjective, but even size also appears to be so. George Berkeley illustrated this point concerning size by asking us to picture a mite. We cannot even see a tiny mite, yet something that either possesses more precise vision or is of corresponding size can. The latter is an important point: size is heavily influenced by perspective. For a mite, a cat is enormous, but for a human, it is an average-sized animal. Even a spider is large for a mite though small for a human. A bear viewed from far away appear quite small, but up close it is large. In each case the stimuli are the same but perspective results in vastly different experiences. The same is true of taste, smell, and touch.

In each case, our experience of sound, sight, taste, smell, and physical sensation are all mental phenomena apparently caused by external stimuli but which do not correspond to that physical stimuli. This lack of correspondence is witnessed in the different experiences of those who receive the same perception, or the ability for the mind to misinterpret such external stimuli (leading us to believe light reflected from hot asphalt is water, for example). After carefully examining our senses, we must conclude that our experience is not a bare representation of the external world (a position called naïve realism): it is an interpretation of all sorts of apparently external stimuli. Our minds receive one thing and present to us another. This initial observation does not necessarily lead to scepticism: instead, we can marvel at the amazing complexity of the world God has created. It is mindboggling that our experience involves the perfectly synchronized interaction of external reality, physical senses, and mental interpretation. However, it does caution us against thinking that there is a one-to-one correlation between our experience and the external world. Indeed, it is impossible to imagine what the external world is actually like: if depth, proportion, shape, texture, colour, smell, taste, and touch are all the result of a careful balance of stimuli, reception, and interpretation, then the world before interpretation is impossible to imagine! Many studies have gone further to identify the variegated way interpretation "creates" the world we perceive: interpretation is not objective but is informed by our God-given faculties along with our conscious and tacit beliefs, so that in many ways we see the world as we want to see it.

Where does this leave us? At this point, some philosophers have dismissed the external world entirely (with sceptical or theistic conclusions offered in its place), or they have decried the pursuit of knowledge of the external world at all. However, we do not need to follow these paths. On the one hand, the "external world" is really not so external: it is a complex reality that involves interpretation in its creation but is, nevertheless, not subjective because of this. We reject subjectivity for two reasons: first, the world has been pre-interpreted by God, so there is a "right" interpretation or mental construction of the external world. Second, because God has structured the world and our senses that we may have knowledge of it and thrive within it for his glory, we can trust that our faculties offer us the world as we are meant to perceive it, at least they do so when functioning correctly. "Meant to perceive it" is not the world without perception at all: we have no reason to believe we were ever meant to know the world apart from perception. Instead, we have every reason to believe that God carefully constructed the creation so that it would be a coherent equilibrium between the unconstructed world and the constructing mind, working in tandem to present the "real," or the world of our experience. In many ways this is a team effort, for the fact that God has granted functioning faculties to humanity as a whole does not guarantee that every human possesses them: our experience abounds with evidence to the contrary. Some people experience physical impairment, others mental impairment, still others experience momentary impairment from physical trauma or substance abuse. However, working together, we can discern where malformed experience is occurring and submit to the judgment of others who are not experiencing the same distortions as we are. This is true not only of our basic faculties but also our belief systems.

In many ways, we see what we believe we will see. For example, if we are committed to the belief that resurrections are impossible, we will intuitively arrive at alternate conclusions when confronted with an apparent resurrection. Believing rightly is an important part of seeing rightly, as we saw in *The Gift of Knowing*. Therefore, we need others. Most importantly, we need God to construct the world of experience accurately. By submitting to others in our weakness and submitting to God as he has revealed himself in his Word, we can have confidence that we will see the world as he has intended us to see it and so be able to respond as he has intended us to respond.

All I have hoped to achieve in this chapter is raise the problem: our world is an interpreted world. There is no such thing as neutrality or objectivity. In addition, I have attempted to move us away from the conclusion that a lack of neutrality or objectivity leaves us with scepticism. God gives us a way beyond pure subjectivity, a way to uphold truth. It is to this that we must now turn.

Further Reading

George Berkeley, *Principles of Human Knowledge* [A]
George Berkeley, *Three Dialogues* [A][1]
*John Frame, *The Doctrine of the Knowledge of God* [B-I]
David Hume, *An Enquiry into the Human Understanding* [A][2]
Iain McGilchrist, *The Master and His Emissary* [A][3]
*Esther Meek, *Longing to Know* [B]
Esther Meek, *Loving to Know* [I][4]
*Michael Polanyi, *Personal Knowledge: Towards a Post-Critical Philosophy* [A]
*Michael Polanyi, *The Tacit Dimension* [I][5]
Sickler, Bradley L, *God on the Brain* [B]

---

[1] *Principles* is a highly abstract work. Berkeley wrote the *Three Dialogues* to present his main argument for subjective idealism in a more accessible and persuasive manner.

[2] *The Enquiry* summarises the main argument of Hume's larger *A Treatise on Human Nature* but is still a difficult work for those without a philosophical background.

[3] McGilchrist presents a fascinating account of the recent literature on the brain and the way it construes the world. I am not persuaded by his conclusions, and he is heavily influenced by the philosophical traditions of Phenomenalism and Existentialism, which I believe are extremely unhelpful. However, the book is fascinating and, for our purposes, presents the data for the subjectivity of experience persuasively. See my review, https://teleioteti.ca/2020/10/29/review-of-the-master-and-his-emissary/.

[4] See my review, https://teleioteti.ca/2020/11/18/review-of-loving-to-know/.

[5] In *Personal Knowledge* and *The Tacit Dimension*, Polanyi agrees that objective knowledge is impossible, our minds are actively involved in presenting us the world we perceive in experience. However, this does not mean we cannot have truth or know the world outside of us. *Personal Knowledge* has many profound insights but settles on a decidedly unconvincing account of truth as personal assent. *The Tacit Dimension* presents many of what I would judge to be the most important theses in *Personal Knowledge* in an easier manner.

TRUTH: THE FIRST INTERPRETER

Once again, the answer to the critical questions of ontology is seen to be Yahweh, the living God. He furnishes the world with continuous identity (Part 1), he created the worlds diversity while maintaining its unity through his interpreting word (Part 2), and he has created both the world that causes perception and the world of perception so that we might adequately perceive his world (Part 3). What remains for our purposes is to explore the last dimensions of God's work to ontologically sustain creation. Ontology, however it has been pursued, has concerned itself with truth. The philosophers have sought to identify the adequate objects of knowledge and the nature of that knowledge. In the Christian tradition, the view of truth as correspondence with reality has dominated. However, this view has relied on either Platonism, where truth is restricted to the world of the Forms and is a correspondence between human speech and the Forms, or objective empiricism, where there is somehow a correspondence between knowledge and the extra-mental world (the nature of mental content and so knowledge for such a position has been debated heavily). Our argument thus far has ruled out both these positions, but we need not give in to the sceptical alternatives. Our argument thus far gives a better ground for truth than either of these positions, namely, God himself.

As Van Til repeatedly stated throughout his life, there is no un-interpreted or brute fact.[1] Every facet of the creation is known and interpreted—given

---

[1] E.g. *A Christian Theory of Knowledge.*

value, meaning, and purpose—by God. God has pre-interpreted all things, so knowledge is merely thinking God's thoughts after him, and truth is a correspondence (however partial and finite) between our interpretation and his. Now, there will always be a qualitative difference between our thoughts and his, such that his are prior and ours follow, his create what they interpret and ours respond to his creation, his are the norm and our are normed. Nevertheless, there is a genuine correspondence. God is truth, as is his spoken Word: God's thoughts are the standard of truth itself by which any human thought is measured. What we have seen in this book is the extent to which this is true. God's thoughts uphold individual identity, so they are the standard for our perception of continuity. God's thoughts have exhausted every relation between himself and the creation and every created thing to everything else, thus acting as the standard for all universal concepts. Finally, the world itself exists to some extent as a mental construct. However, the real is not, therefore, purely subjective and relative, for it has always existed as it was meant to be perceived in God's interpretation. All thought, every perception, and each experience are wholly interpretative. Our interpretation is true when it corresponds to God's. However, "knowledge" is a complex thing, so how this works is complicated. We will consider here only three facets of knowledge, propositional knowledge, person-knowledge (with its analogues), and conceptual knowledge.

a. Propositional Knowledge

As far as classic philosophy was concerned, knowledge had one form, propositions. A proposition is a statement with, minimally, a subject and a predicate: "he is," for example. For Plato and Aristotle, knowledge concerned abstract things and the laws that governed their relations. A law can be expressed propositionally, e.g. when X then Y, as can the definition of a thing, e.g. a human is a rational animal. Logic, for Aristotle, governed the way we speak and reason about things. For the Stoics (another group of Greek philosophers), knowledge was still propositional but this time concerned states of affairs (e.g. it is raining). They developed a logic for relating propositions of this sort. In our view, Aristotle's view of logic is problematic, for there is no abstract definition of anything, and terms do not have the clear-cut boundaries that his logic requires (though his insights are still very

THE GIFT OF SEEING

valuable).[2] Propositional knowledge, especially in the Stoic sense, remains important in the biblical perspective. The Bible asserts many truths that are or may be articulated in propositional form (e.g. Jesus was crucified; Jesus rose again). A proposition may be true or false, but truth requires a standard or norm. However, unlike the Platonists, we have rejected the existence of abstract forms, so a statement such as "a human has a mind" is not true with reference to an abstract definition, a "form." Instead, several conditions relate to the truth or falsity of this statement. First, it is true if and only if the group of particulars indicated by the term "human" all possess "mind." Second, it may be true in one context and false in another. If uttered by Stan, who cognizes rocks with humans in his concept of "human," this statement is false. However, if such a statement were found in the Bible, where all "humans" (אָדָם, אִישׁ, אֱנוֹשׁ, ἄνθρωπος) possess a mind, it would be true. No such statement is thus categorically true, but is true or false depending on a given context. God has pre-interpreted all reality, including human cognition and utterance, so his mind is the standard by which any statement is made true or false. Similarly, in the case of states of affairs ("it is raining"), all such propositions are both temporally and subjectively contingent; that is, "raining" is dependent on a person's concept of rain (subjective) and is time-stamped (it is only true or false with reference to time and place). Thus, such a proposition is an interpretation of a particular experience and is made true or false with reference to God's interpretation. God's interpretation is, in this way, the truth-maker for all propositions. The objective truth status of a proposition is a different matter than its subjective status, as belief or knowledge. God's interpretation *makes* something true, but how can we be confident or justified in believing that it us true?

Several factors are at play in this question, namely, correspondence, coherence, and functionality. First, our belief must correspond to our experience *as created by right-functioning faculties*. That is, not all experiences warrant belief. Experiences derived from physical or mental handicaps or from temporary distortion (e.g. being high on drugs) or influenced by any other mechanism which causes false beliefs (such as

---

[2] Cf. Vern S. Poythress, *Logic: A God-Centered Approach to the Foundation of Western Thought*, Electronic. (Wheaton: Crossway, 2013).

illusion) are not a sufficient basis for belief. As discussed above, our faculties are basically trustworthy, but we need two or three "witnesses" (Deut 19:15) to confirm the reliability of our subjective interpretation. Thus, justified belief corresponds to experience for which we have good reason to trust (the basic trustworthiness of our faculties and the principle of external attestation, two or three witnesses). However, our physical/mental faculties are only one factor in interpretation: interpretation involves reading the world in light of our prior beliefs.

Thus, a justified belief must cohere with our worldview, or better, the correct worldview. Subjectively, if we are aware of tension, such a belief is not justified. For the most part, our worldview interacts with the world on an implicit level, so we are intuitively aware of contradictions, and our experience or framework is adjusted accordingly. However, there are times where we become consciously aware of dissonance, at which time a belief is justified when it coheres with our conscious beliefs. However, not any worldview will do: because God has revealed himself, we are obligated to bring our beliefs in line with his Word, so justification depends on coherence with a biblically shaped worldview or, in other words, the Bible's interpretation of everything.

Finally, a justified belief is functional. The belief that disease is unreal is not justified because it is unliveable: a person cannot consistently live with this belief. A proposition is true when it corresponds with God's interpretation; we believe it is true when it confirms with attested experience, a biblically shaped worldview, and life as informed by the Bible and experience. God is thus essential for truth making and subjective justification, for his Word gives us necessary access to the appropriate worldview for interpreting the world and the assurance that our faculties are basically reliable. Propositional knowledge is important, but it is neither the only nor the most common form of knowledge in our experience or in the Bible. More common, more important, is person-knowledge, or the knowledge of persons.

b. Person-Knowledge

Think of the statement, "I know X," where X represents any person, such as your mother, father, spouse, or friend. Clearly, the knowledge in question is not propositional knowledge—or at least it is not merely propositional knowledge. My claim to know Nicole, my wife, is not a claim to know the definition of the word "Nicole," nor any state of affair pertaining to Nicole. Yet, what is in view is certainly knowledge. Moreover, it is not less than propositional knowledge. That is, if I knew nothing about Nicole, such as her relationship status, family, anything about her, or any fact about her life, my claim to know her would certainly be false. However, no enumerated list of propositions can encompass my knowledge of Nicole. This knowledge is not only past but present; it informs my thoughts and actions towards her. This knowledge is also future-oriented, allowing me to anticipate her actions and feelings in countless circumstances. This is what I call person-knowledge.[3]

Before we explore the concept further, it is interesting to observe that person-knowledge extends beyond human and divine, even spiritual, persons—so perhaps I need to think of a better name for it! The closest analogue is the knowledge of animals: we know pets in an analogous way to our knowledge of persons. We may anticipate their future actions and decipher their present condition in terms of deep understanding of them. (There may be a similar but weaker analogy with our interactions with certain things, where we attribute significance that is not intrinsic to the thing (such as a child's pet rock); I am not yet convinced of this.)

Once we acknowledge that this is a form of knowing distinct from propositional knowledge, we are struck by three facts. First, this sort of knowledge is common in the Bible; second, this is the most common form of knowledge in our everyday lives; third, it is a form of knowledge neglected by the ancient philosophers. As for its commonness, every interaction with a familiar person involves it—and new interactions involve its development. Furthermore, we talk about knowing this or that person very frequently. In the Bible, propositional knowledge is often rendered with a particle indicating a state of affairs, knowing *that*. At other times, the words meaning "to know" (e.g. יָדַע, γινώσκω, ἐπιγνώσκω) have a direct object, indicating propositional

---

[3] I am avoiding "personal knowledge" despite its parallelism with "propositional knowledge" because "personal" suggests subjectivity and in his influential book *Personal Knowledge*, Michael Polanyi intends by "personal" the intricate subjective involvement of persons in every act of knowing. His work is of immense value but is not what I intend. Polanyi, *Personal Knowledge*.

knowledge (knowing the content associated with that object, e.g. "he knew the word [= what was said"]), an experience associated with the object, or conceptual knowledge, which we will consider below. However, the use of "know" with a personal subject, e.g. "He knew Yahweh," has distinct connotations. In many cases, to know a person of the opposite sex indicates sexual relations (e.g. Gen 4:1, 17, 25; Matt 1:25), and in non-sexual contexts, it often indicates an established relationship (e.g. Rom 8:29, 11:2). Thus, for the most part, the use of the term "to know" with a person in the Bible implies what I am calling person-knowledge but explicitly indicates a positive relationship with the person knowing (e.g. Gen 18:19, 29:5; 2 Sam 7:20; Isa 19:21; Matt 7:23; John 10:15, 27; Rom 8:29, 11:2).[4] To know Yahweh includes person-knowledge but also a commitment to Yahweh and the positive response to that knowledge. In English, we often speak of knowing a person without explicitly indicating a relationship (I may know someone who hates me). The Bible occasionally does so; for instance, Nathaniel expresses shock that Jesus knew him (John 1:48). Of Saul, those who "knew him previously" were shocked when he prophesied with a group of prophets (1 Sam 10:11). This seems to be the sense of Psalm 138:6b: God sees and so attends to the righteous, but he has no relationship with the wicked. Furthermore, as Christians, we come to know God (e.g. 1 John 2:3, 13), but all humans know God despite acting contrary to this knowledge (Rom 1:21). Thus, the use of "know" with the connotations of positive, intimate relationship seems to be a deeper extension of the basic sense of person-knowledge. This is particularly prominent with reference to God, who knows all people (e.g. John 2:24-25) and yet knows some people in a unique way (Matt 7:23; John 10:27; Rom 8:29, 11:2; 1 John 2:3, 13).

What, then, do we make of person-knowledge, this important but neglected form of understanding? I believe that it is closely connected to what I have called earlier "interiority," closely related to but not identical with "mind." The modern world is the age of the interior or the self; it is in the Modern and Post-Modern eras that the idea of interiority or the self has received the most attention and analysis. The self is the subjective centre of

---

[4] Matt 7:16-20, John 1:48 may be an instance where person-knowledge is intended but a relationship is not implied.

a person, the "I." That is, neither you nor I can be reduced to our bodies, senses, or brain activity. There are instruments for measuring our brain activity, neural activity, and different aspects of our physical nature, yet no matter how exhaustive the analysis, this data does not begin to approach what it means to be "me" or to explain my experience.

Part of self is consciousness, the awareness of a body as "ours" and the world in distinction from us.[5] Part of the self is identity, our perception of ourselves in relation to and in distinction from other persons, the perception that though similar in appearance, I think, act, and have different experiences from other humans. Part of the self is knowledge and memory, accumulated experience and belief. I do not intend to give an exhaustive definition of the "self"—indeed, I believe that is impossible—but I hope this sketch of several features of the self indicate what I mean. So, by interiority I mean the subjective "I." The "I" is interior in that it is not visible nor exhaustively known to any other created being: it is distinctly mine.

Furthermore, it is not exhausted by the self; it is interior as our organs are interior, inextricably linked to everyday functioning and yet invisible. What I have called "mind" is one aspect of the self: "mind" describes the self in terms of transcendence, not bound by the cause-effect order of the physical realm. In the same way, I would describe the "body" as another perspective on or aspect of the self: the body is not something we "possess," merely an instrument as alien to us as a car or pen. Instead, our body is precisely ourselves as they are subject to the cause-effect immanence of the physical world. Mind and Body are thus not two different things, entirely distinct, nor the same thing (as physicalism would have it): instead, they are two essential ways of considered one thing, the self, considered as in the world (body) and above the world (mind).[6] When we speak of identity, character, morality,

---

[5] This should not be taken for granted: it has been well established that different forms of brain trauma can cause someone to lose the sense of connection between the self and the body, indicating both the interconnectedness between the brain and the self and the distinction between us as our embodied whole and us as the experiencing subject. Cf. McGilchrist, *The Master and His Emissary*; Polanyi, *Personal Knowledge*, 1–17, 49–248.

[6] I have benefited from but make no effort to follow the discussion of the human constitution in John M. Frame, *Systematic Theology: An Introduction to Christian Belief* (Phillipsburg: P&R Publishing, 2013), sec. 7.34.D-E.

habit, knowledge, memory, values, beliefs, relationships, etc., we are speaking of the self. The fact that we can and do speak of this interiority indicates that it is not unknown to ourselves nor others. How then, if it is suprasensible (more than we can access through our senses), do we come to know a "person"?

Thomas Aquinas once described our knowledge of God, given that his essence was supposed to be inaccessible to us, knowledge of his effects.[7] I think Aquinas is wrong to give epistemological priority to the essence, as we have seen earlier in this book, and I think he is also wrong to separate the two as if knowing the effects of something can be separated from knowing the thing itself. But by drawing attention to the subject's activities as an avenue of knowledge (as Basil of Caesarea had done before him), Aquinas brings us close to the answer of how we know a person. We know persons like we know the wind: we cannot see it, but we see its effects everywhere. We feel it and experience its consequences.

In the same way, I can only directly perceive the external part of Nicole's self. Yet, through her expressions, actions, and words in various circumstances, a door is opened to her interiority. I begin to grasp the core that makes her who she is. As I grow in relationship with her, I begin to interpret her external behaviour in terms of her interiority. I can identify what is characteristic and out-of-character. I can identify habits and help her to overcome bad ones. I can discern subtle emotions that are not evident to others, associating subtle physical characteristics with her interior disposition.

The fascinating thing about person-knowledge is that it can be mediated over time and distance (even reality) through various visual and audio mediums. We can read the letters and books of historical figures and come to know them: we can anticipate why they did this or that and what they might have said or how they might have responded in another circumstance.[8]

---

[7] Thomas Aquinas, *Summa Contra Gentiles* (2 XI-XII).

[8] Now, some critics take this too far and assume they can know with great precision the thought life and motivations of historical authors. There is great danger in pushing the partial knowledge we can access in literature. C.S. Lewis has some apt words on the subject in an essay in *Christian Reflections*. We could clarify that the person we come to know through literature is an "implied" person, who may or may

There is a degree of danger in overreading this sort of mediated person-knowledge into history, but we experience the same thing through various mediums of communication, such as video, SMS, email, letter, etc. Strange enough, when a novelist creates a compelling character, the reader acquires something analogous to person-knowledge, coming to anticipate that character's response in all sorts of circumstances.[9] Person-knowledge is fascinating and complex, yet essential to social life and self-understanding.

A key presupposition of this book has been that knowledge of God is presented in Scripture as this sort of knowledge: to know God is to know God as a person. I believe this claim needs little argument because it arises naturally from reading the biblical story and makes terrific sense of the Bible's insistence that we truly know God. It also explains why knowing God is a frequent refrain throughout Scripture that involves relational connotations without explicit (or with only minimal) propositional content.

We are discussing knowledge in relation to truth, so important questions are raised by person-knowledge: can it be true or false? what would this mean? It is undoubtedly the case that person-knowledge can be true or false. That is, if I claim to know Nicole and yet I am unable to understand or relate to her, that claim is surely false. However, there is a significant degree of variability between truth and falsehood when it comes to person-knowledge: I may know Stan to a certain degree, but not nearly as well as I know Nicole. My claim to know either is *true*, but the truth of this knowledge does not tell much about its degree. Furthermore, as the interiority of any person is unconscious to themselves, so our person-knowledge is unconsciousness to us. That is, I certainly know Nicole, but I cannot enumerate what that means—at least not to any exhaustive degree. Yet my knowledge is evident

---

not an accurate presentation of the real person. Cf. C. S. Lewis, "Modern Theology and Biblical Criticism," in *Christian Reflections* (Eerdmans, 1967), 152–166; Jean Louis Ska, *"Our Fathers Have Told Us": Introduction to the Analysis of Hebrew Narratives*, Subsidia Biblica 13 (Roma: Editrice Pontificio Instituto Biblico, 1990), 41; J. Alexander Rutherford, *God's Kingdom through His Priest-King: An Analysis of the Book of Samuel in Light of the Davidic Covenant*, Teleioteti Technical Studies 1 (Vancouver: Teleioteti, 2019), 115–116. Cf. Tom Kindt and Hans-Harald Müller, *The Implied Author: Concept and Controversy* (Walter de Gruyter, 2008).

[9] Cf. John M. Frame, *The Doctrine of God*, A Theology of Lordship (Phillipsburg: P&R Publishing, 2002), 156–159.

from the way we relate to one another. For his reason, I conclude that person-knowledge functions at a *tacit* level, part of the interpretive matrix we bring to the world. Person-knowledge is not the sort of knowledge we analyse and logically parse; instead, is the sort of knowledge that shapes our interpretation of our experience, constructs the world, and governs our behaviour (both intuitively and reflectively). In the latter case, when we consciously reflect on our relationship with and actions towards a person we know, we draw on person-knowledge without ever grasping the whole. Like an iceberg, we may access the tip of the knowledge we possess in rational processes but cannot discern the depths of the knowledge we possess. Once again, this account of person-knowledge fits remarkably well with Paul's account of the innate knowledge of God all persons have (Romans 1:18-3:20).

In the case of person-knowledge, it would appear at first glance that the truth-maker of our knowledge claim is a person's interiority. However, this raises several problems. First, the future-immortality of persons (that the righteous and the unrighteous will endure beyond physical death, be resurrected, and live forever) means that in any situation where we may know a person, there will always be a truth-maker, namely, the existing self. However, two problems emerge at this point: first, it would be impossible on this account to know a future self who has not yet existed; second, all such knowledge would carry an implicit time statement. In the first case, if the person themself makes a knowledge claim true (i.e. "I know Nicole" is true because my knowledge truly corresponds to Nicole's self), then knowledge of that person is impossible when they do not exist. Of course, the problem this raises is for God's foreknowledge, and it contradicts the explicit claims of Scripture (e.g. Jer 1:5; Rom 8:29; 11:2): God's knowledge could not be true on this account, for there was no truth-maker until that person was born. Second, "I know Nicole" would only be true for a moment, after which it would only be true that I knew Nicole. That is, if the truth-maker of my claim is Nicole herself, she is constantly changing. I may have known her on March 29th, 2021, but she has changed by March 30th, 2021. Several qualifications are, therefore, necessary.

First, no person-knowledge claim made by humans is an exhaustive claim: to say "I know Nicole" is not to say I have comprehended her interiority but that I know her well enough for the relationship I profess to have with her.

Such truth claims are always claims to a degree and the truth of the statement depends on the relationship to which that claim pertains (to say one knows the grocery store cashier requires far less tacit content than to say one knows one's spouse). Only in the case of God's knowledge of persons is such a claim exhaustive. However, this does not threaten our knowledge of one another, so it should not threaten our knowledge of God. That is, that I only know Nicole to the degree appropriate for our relationship does not deny the veracity of my claim in any way. Similarly, that I know God only so much as he has permitted and as is appropriate for our relationship does not in any way deny the veracity of my claim. Thus, the unbeliever and believer both know God in truth, though the degree of that knowledge is relative to their relationship with him.

Second, as with propositional knowledge and (as we will see) concept-knowledge, we must confess that person-knowledge is always an interpretation to any degree it exists. That is, my knowledge of Nicole is not an image of her interiority. I have no experience of what she experiences, with the particular inflections of her faculties and beliefs. Interiority is a complex of physical and mental operations, faculties, causes, etc. not recreated or mirrored in my person-knowledge, not even partially. Indeed, interiority is not reproduced even in a person's self-knowledge. Interiority, as observed above, is the consciousness, unconsciousness, and physicality of the body working in unison. As with every other aspect of reality, interiority is part extra-mental and part mental. A person's consciousness or mind is their interpretation of themselves; my tacit knowledge of that person is another interpretation of that same reality.

Thus, as with all other knowledge, the truth-maker for person-knowledge is God's exhaustive interpretation of a person, his knowledge of their own subjectivity and the reality that it interprets. My claim to know Nicole is true in as much as it partially but faithfully corresponds to God's exhaustive interpretation of Nicole, reflected faithfully in her own subjectivity. There is true continuity in Nicole's identity across time, represented by God's interpretation, her own subjectivity, and the extra-mental reality, such that my claim is always true though it never exhausts Nicole at all times nor at any one time. Given this account, we can resolve the first dilemma raised above concerning God's foreknowledge.

If the truth-maker is God's interpretation, then it predates the creation of everything, including that person. That is, if a person's subjectivity is their own interpretation of the complex of mind and body, thus being only a perspective on their self or interiority and not the interiority itself, it is not independent of the extra-mental reality which God has created. Moreover, because subjectivity is itself an interpretation of the self, the two are closely tied together, but the former can exist without the latter. For example, in a coma or deep sleep, the self still exists even if subjectivity is absent. God's exhaustive knowledge of the extra-subjective self allows him to know our subjectivity exhaustively, even before we experience it. Therefore, every person existed potentially in God's plan for creation and thus existed as an object of God's contemplation and interpretation alongside impersonal creation, like rocks, laws, and water. Therefore, person-knowledge is dependent on God's eternal plan and pre-interpretation.

Before turning to the final aspect of knowledge we will contemplate, conceptual knowledge, it is worth observing a rather unexpected conclusion that arises from the above discussion. Above, I drew attention to the analogy that obtains between a real person and a fictional character: both may be an object of person-knowledge. A well-written character takes on a life of their own, such that the author is not free to make of them whatever they will but are constrained by their initial vision for the character: once a character is established as faithful and true, God-fearing, and close to his family, it is incredulous that the same character would be portrayed as an atheist adulterer. We would cry foul! Either the original portrayal was *false*—and so the plot is perhaps a complex and psychologically provoking work—or the author has broken faith; they have broken the rules of good literature. Perhaps all that separates a good character in fiction and a real person is subjectivity, the ability to *experience* what is going on. One might object, what about free will! Free will is itself a complex issue; John Frame has tried to explain it on analogy with a narrative.[10]

Calvinists have long wrestled with the apparent tension between divine sovereignty and human responsibility, which the World (and various Christian theologies) call a contradiction. Their answer has been a position called compatibilism: compatibilism claims that free will really means humans

---

[10] Ibid.

are responsible for their actions and that responsibility is not contradicted by God's exhaustive sovereignty. I go to great length addressing this issue in my book *Prevenient Grace*, but it is important to consider the matter here.[11] For many, compatibilism means that free will means freedom from coercion: I am free when I do what I desire and I am not forced to do something. Things get complicated when we consider different kinds of desire, but this holds true despite the complexity.[12] Thus, freedom is linked with the subjectivity of a person, not the determinism of their circumstances (which the Bible tells us is exhaustive). Before the world was created, God ordained every single event that would happen. He planned and knew everything that would happen, as an author plans and knows everything about their novel. However, we know that God's determinism does not eliminate subjectivity or responsibility.

Following John Frame, we can picture this on analogy with the expert novelist: God foreknew every person he would make and created them as distinct persons. Given that personhood is an objective reality underlying a person's subjectivity, he could write their life's story without every violating the integrity of his vision for their personhood. On the one hand, they do what they do because God ordained for them to do it; on the other hand, they do what they do because they genuinely want to and make the subjective choice to do so. This may be a disconcerting thought at first. However, it coheres with the biblical vision of the compatibility of sovereignty and human responsibility. It also arises naturally out of our account of personhood or interiority and our knowledge of this reality.

c. Conceptual Knowledge

All that is left in our investigation of ontology on the biblical account is our knowledge of concepts, or conceptual knowledge. Conceptual knowledge is not propositional knowledge, for it cannot be expressed in a proposition

---

[11] Cf. J. Alexander Rutherford, *Prevenient Grace: An Investigation into Arminianism*, 2nd Revised Ed., Teleioteti Technical Studies 2 (Vancouver: Teleioteti, 2020).

[12] Concerning complexity, in one sense, I do not desire to give my life for my family, but in another I do and would, so though it conflicts with desire in one sense, I am still free when I make that choice

(discussed in Chapter 6), nor is it person-knowledge, for it concerns many things and not any one person. In one sense, I would question whether it is rightly called *knowledge*, but we will see that this is true in a sense. That is, if a concept is primarily a mental act or habitual event for relating particulars, it is less like a proposition or that tacit interpretation of a person than it is like muscle memory or another habit by which we automatically respond to external and internal stimuli. Furthermore, it is hard to see how such an act can be true or false: if our mind draws two things into relation, then the concept of these things depends on their similarity, even if this similarity is minute. If a concept exists, it somehow corresponds to things, however useless this correspondence might be. Thus, concepts as mental habits may be more or less useful but are not true or false. However, we saw above that there is another perspective to be taken on concepts. A concept also refers to the relationship drawn between similar things: thus, I may have a concept which is the habit of relating all things with a similar colour; by calling this concept "redness," I isolate this relationship as an object of thought. It is in this sense that a concept is an object of knowledge. My thoughts *about* redness will be propositional and follow the rules identified above. However, the conceptual relationship will exist on the tacit level of interpretation, allowing me to interpret this or that object as red, a dog, a beagle, even if I cannot articulate what it means to be "red," a "dog," or a "beagle" in propositions. This implicit component of a concept is a form of knowledge employed in everyday life, even if it is rarely an object of direct thought.

This conceptual knowledge may be true or false in as much as the relationship that constitutes the concept actually obtains between all the objects of relevance. As discussed below, truth and falsehood with reference to concepts emerge primarily in the context of communication. That is, if my concept of "dog" builds on physical similarity, it may be false to include a human in that concept. It is possible for my concept of "dog" to include all the members of another concept, "human," in which case, the proposition "a human is a dog" would be true. However, if communicated in the context where humans were implicitly excluded from the concept dog, as with specific reference to the physiology of dogs, the proposition a "human is a dog" would be false, as would be the concept of "dog" that includes both humans and the idea of form or physical similarity. Of course, we could use the term "dog" for a concept that encompasses what we would conventionally call dogs and humans, but such a concept would only be true if it excluded the close similarity of form shared by "dogs" but not by "humans and dogs." It may be better to call the "truth" of a concept as accuracy, which sounds more natural to my ears. However, for our purposes, a concept is true when it rightly denotes a relationship obtaining between objects. Because that "relationship" only exists in mental interpretation, every concept is known to God and receives its truth value from him. Where the relationship is accurate, such that our concept corresponds to some extent without falsehood to God's pre-interpreted concepts, then that concept is true. Where this correspondence is not valid, then a concept is false.

Because concepts arise from habitual acts and are a tacit framework for relating objects, it unlikely that falsehood would emerge unintentionally. Given the basic trustworthiness of our faculties, attested in an individual's case by the presence of knowing community ("two or three witnesses"), we have every reason to believe our concepts to be true. However, when it comes to naming and communicating concepts, unintentional and intentional falsehood may enter. As it regards unintentional falsehood, if I use the term "dog" to communicate a concept of objects others call "books," I am liable to be misinterpreted. My choice of a sign, "d-o-g," has facilitated this falsehood. We could also unintentionally arrive at a false concept by misunderstanding a book. Thus, to facilitate communication, it is necessary to attend to the conventions of a given culture, to use the appropriate language in communication, and to read the works of others carefully in order to understand them and deal with them fairly.

Intentional falsehood may emerge because there is much rhetorical power in the use of concepts. For example, grouping a local pastor whom we dislike with those commonly recognized as false teachers amounts to portraying that pastor as a false teacher. If this were not the case, the attribution would be slanderous and the concept false. Calling certain humans "animals" or "barbarians" over against the rest of humanity would be similar, as would identifying unborn children as something other than persons, babies, or other terms that invoke the continuity between unborn and born life. Thus, in philosophy, when someone intentionally expounds the relationships between things, or in rhetoric, the possibility for false concepts is strong. However, where there is truth, it only exists because God has first thought it. All thought, conscious or unconscious, thus relies on the God who has pre-interpreted all things, created us to know as he has known, and revealed himself so that we might do so.

Further Reading

Michael Polanyi, *Personal Knowledge* [I-A]
*Michael Polanyi, *The Tacit Dimension* [I-A]
*John Frame, *The Doctrine of the Knowledge of God* [I]
John Frame, *The Doctrine of God* [I]
*John Frame, *Apologetics: A Justification of Christian Belief* [B-I]
Iain McGilchrist, *The Master and His Emissary: The Divided Brain and the Making of the Western World* [A]
Esther Meek, *Loving to Know: Introducing Covenant Epistemology* [B-I]
Vern Poythress, *Logic: A God-Centered Approach to the Foundation of Western Thought* [A]
Bradley L. Sickler, *God on the Brain* [B]

CONCLUSION

The fear of the LORD is the beginning of wisdom, and the knowledge of the Holy One is insight. – Proverbs 9:10

He is the radiance of the glory of God and the exact imprint of his nature, and he upholds the universe by the word of his power. – Hebrews 1:2

We set out in this book to investigate ontology from a biblical perspective. We did not do so for the sake of knowledge itself; instead, we did so because ontology has historically been a critical battleground for Christian theology. It has frequently been an area where biblical teaching has come under attack. We have investigated the issue with the conviction that Scripture has something to say and can help us confidently go forth to understand God's word, God's world, and God himself. We approached the subject through three significant problems raised in the history of philosophy: the problems of change and identity, the one and the many, and the external world.

In Part 1, we saw that the concept of history and sense experience raises a problem for knowledge, yet the existence of minds and, more importantly, of the sovereign God who has pre-interpreted all things means that change is not the problem it was thought to be. Instead, change is a good thing in God's plan for creation: change and history are the means through which God has revealed himself to his creation. In Part 2, we considered the problem of the One and the Many. We discovered that the problem did not emerge out of the neutral observation of the world but out of certain preconceptions through which ancient and modern philosophers have interpreted the world. Instead of a problem, we saw that the Bible embraces the utterly contingent or particular world of our experience and that God gives ultimate unity to the world through his intentional, wise ordering or creation and interpretation of it. Finally, in Part 3, we considered the problem of the external world. That is, if our minds have a significant role in presenting the outside world to us, what can we really know about it? We saw that God created the world to exist as the equilibrium between mental interpretation and extra-mental reality. As such, truth never exists outside of the mind, nor do truth-makers. Instead, God is the standard of truth in its various senses and has enabled and continues to uphold our knowledge. Thus, far from being an arid and godless discipline, we have seen that ontology points consistently back to God, the creator of all things.

I believe we have witnessed the truth of the Proverbs, that "The fear of the LORD is the beginning of wisdom, and the knowledge of the Holy One is insight" (Prov 9:10). At each step, the possibility of knowledge is secured by God and our possession of it by his wise ordering of creation. Creation is utterly dependent on God while being distinct from him; it is always the creation, not the creator. Therefore, we are called to engage as creatures in all our knowing, humbled by our sheer dependence on the kindness and mercy of God, our creator. We have seen just a small glimmer of what it means for Jesus our Lord to uphold "the universe by the word of his power" (Heb 1:2).

God spoke all things into existence through his Son (Gen 1-2; John 1:1-5) and sustains its unity and rationality by his decree, pre-interpreting all things and governing the interactions of created things. Moreover, at some point, we discover that the world itself rests on God's word. This is true in the temporal sense: God's word is the cause of things coming into existence. It is also true in another sense. Philosophy and the physical sciences have sought to find the fundamental causes of all things in the natural world, that by which all else is explained. "Laws" orchestrate the ways things interact, but they do not cause the things themselves. There is the standard theory of particle physic in the natural sciences, which probes the causes of all macro-phenomenon at their elementary basis. The behavior of atoms is explained by appeal to their constituent pieces, neutrons, protons, and electrons. These, in turn, are explained by the various more basic elements, such as quarks, supposed to explain their properties. At some point, we must arrive at an explanation that is itself not explained by something else. What causes the quarks to vary from one another and gives them their own properties? If these are not the most basic explanation, what explains the substrate that explains them? The answer, whether at the level of the quark or deeper, must at some point be God. He is the only one who can uphold creation without himself being upheld. Thus, his word not only explains the origins of the created world but its present existence: it is his word that explains the most basic elements from which all else derives and for which the material world and its interacting forces depend. Spoken by God, the world is his creation and distinct from him, yet it is dependent on him in every way, past, present and future. Truly, "he upholds the universe by the word of his power" (Prov 9:10). "In him we live and move and have our being" (Acts 17:28).

Our first response can only be worship, crying out with the most powerful created beings, "Holy, Holy, Holy is the LORD of hosts; the whole earth is fully of his glory" (Isa 6:3), and proclaiming his wisdom with Paul,

> Oh, the depth of the riches and wisdom and knowledge of God! How unsearchable are his judgments and how inscrutable his ways! "For who has known the mind of the Lord, or who has been his counselor?" "Or who has given a gift to him that he might be repaid?" For from him and through him and to him are all things. To him be glory forever. Amen. (Rom 11:33-36)

God has made the world with intricate wisdom and made himself known so that we may know, love, and serve him. He calls all people to cast themselves on his mercy shown in Christ Jesus and to pursue him with all their lives. So, we must engage the world with the gifts God has given us for his glory, primarily seen in the expansion of his kingdom through the Church of his Son (Matt 28:18-20). However, for those who would question God's wisdom and think they can interpret the world apart from God who created it, his word is strong:

> Who is this that darkens counsel by words without knowledge?

133

Dress for action like a man;
  I will question you, and you make it known to me.

Where were you when I laid the foundation of the earth?
  Tell me, if you have understanding.
Who determined its measurements—surely you know!
  Or who stretched the line upon it?
On what were its bases sunk,
      or who laid its cornerstone,
  when the morning stars sang together
      and all the sons of God shouted for joy?

Or who shut in the sea with doors
  when it burst out from the womb,
when I made clouds its garment
  and thick darkness its swaddling band,
and prescribed limits for it
  and set bars and doors,
and said, Thus far shall you come, and no farther,
  and here shall your proud waves be stayed'?

Have you commanded the morning since your days began,
      and caused the dawn to know its place,
  that it might take hold of the skirts of the earth,
      and the wicked be shaken out of it?
It is changed like clay under the seal,
  and its features stand out like a garment.
From the wicked their light is withheld,
  and their uplifted arm is broken. (Job 38:2-15)

BIBLIOGRAPHY

Aquinas, Thomas. The Summa Contra Gentiles of Saint Thomas Aquinas: The Second Book. London: Burns, Oates & Washbourne, 1923.

Berkeley, George. Principles of Human Knowledge and Three Dialogues. Edited by Howard Robinson. Oxford World's Classics. Oxford: Oxford University Press, 2009.

Bettcher, Talia Mae. Berkeley: A Guide for the Perplexed. Continuum Guides for the Perplexed. London: Continuum, 2008.

Boehner, Philotheus. "The Realistic Conceptualism of Ockham's Philosophy." In Collected Articles on Ockham, edited by Eligius M. Buytaert. 2nd Ed. Franciscan Institute Publications: Philosophy Series 12. N.Y.: The Franciscan Institute, 1992.

Boersma, Hans. Heavenly Participation: The Weaving of a Sacramental Tapestry. Grand Rapids: Eerdmans, 2011.

———. Nouvelle Théologie and Sacramental Ontology: A Return to Mystery. Oxford ; New York: Oxford University Press, 2009.

Callow, Kathleen. Man and Message: A Guide to Meaning-Based Text Analysis. Lanham, Md: Summer Institute of Linguistics, University Press of America, 1998.

Carter, Craig A. Contemplating God with the Great Tradition: Recovering Trinitarian Classical Theism. Grand Rapids: Baker Academic, 2021.

Clark, Gordon H. Thales to Dewey: A History of Philosophy. Cambridge, Massachusetts: The Riverside Press, 1957.

Courtenay, William J. Ockham and Ockhamism : Studies in the

Dissemination and Impact of His Thought. Studien Und Texte Zur Geistesgeschichte Des Mittelalters. Leiden: Brill, 2008.

Dolezal, James E. God without Parts: Divine Simplicity and the Metaphysics of God's Absoluteness. Eugene, Or: Pickwick Publications, 2011.

Edwards, Jonathan. Freedom of the Will. Mineola, N.Y: Dover Publications, 2012.

Ellis, Nicholas J. "Biblical Exegesis and Linguistics: A Prodigal History." In Linguistics and New Testament Greek: Key Issues in the Current Debate, edited by David Alan Black and Benjamin L Merkle. Grand Rapids: Baker Publishing Group, 2020.

Farris, Joshua R., S. Mark Hamilton, and James S. Spiegel. Idealism and Christian Theology : Idealism and Christianity Volume 1. Idealism and Christianity. New York: Bloomsbury Academic, 2016.

Feuerbach, Ludwig. The Essence of Christianity. Translated by George Eliot. Amherst, New York: Prometheus Books, 2010.

Foster, M. B. "The Christian Doctrine of Creation and the Rise of Modern Natural Science." Mind 43, no. 172 (1934): 446–468.

Frame, John M. A History of Western Philosophy and Theology. Phillipsburg: P&R Publishing, 2015.

———. Apologetics: A Justification of Christian Belief. Edited by Joseph E. Torres. Second edition. Phillipsburg, New Jersey: P&R Publishing, 2015.

———. Cornelius Van Til: An Analysis of His Thought. Phillipsburg: P&R Publishing, 1995.

———. Systematic Theology: An Introduction to Christian Belief. Phillipsburg: P&R Publishing, 2013.

———. The Doctrine of God. A Theology of Lordship. Phillipsburg: P&R Publishing, 2002.

———. The Doctrine of the Knowledge of God. A Theology of Lordship. Phillipsburg: P&R Publishing, 1987.

———. Van Til: The Theologian. Phillipsburg: Pilgrim Publishing Company, 1976.

———. "Why Theology Needs Philosophy." In John Frame's Selected Shorter Writings. Vol. 2. Phillipsburg: P&R Pub, 2014.

Grayling, A. C. "Berkeley's Argument for Immaterialism." In The Cambridge Companion to Berkeley, edited by Kenneth Winkler, 166–189. Cambridge companions to philosophy. Cambridge ; New York: Cambridge University Press, 2005.

Hume, David. A Treatise of Human Nature. Edited by L. A. Selby-Bigge. The Clarendon Press, 1888.

———. An Enquiry Concerning Human Understanding. Edited by Tom L. Beauchamp. Oxford Philosophical Texts. Oxford: Oxford University Press, 1999.

———. Dialogues Concerning Natural Religion. Dover Philosophical Classics. Mineola, N.Y.: Dover Publications, 2006.

Kähler, Martin. The So-Called Historical Jesus and the Historic, Biblical Christ. Vancouver: Regent College Pub., 1998.

Kindt, Tom, and Hans-Harald Müller. The Implied Author: Concept and Controversy. Walter de Gruyter, 2008.

Kirschhock, Maximilian E., Helen M. Ditz, and Andreas Nieder. "Behavioral and Neuronal Representation of Numerosity Zero in the Crow." Journal of Neuroscience 41, no. 22 (June 2, 2021): 4889–4896.

Lewis, C. S. "Modern Theology and Biblical Criticism." In Christian Reflections, 152–166. Eerdmans, 1967.

Lowney, Charles and The Polanyi Society. "From Epistemology to Ontology to Epistemontology:" Tradition and Discovery: The Polanyi Society Periodical 40, no. 1 (2013): 16–29.

McGilchrist, Iain. The Master and His Emissary: The Divided Brain and the Making of the Western World. New expanded edition. New Haven: Yale University Press, 2019.

Meek, Esther L. Longing to Know. Grand Rapids: Brazos Press, 2003.

———. Loving to Know: Introducing Covenant Epistemology. Eugene, Ore: Cascade Books, 2011.

Moleski, Martin X. and The Polanyi Society. "Polanyi vs. Kuhn: Worldviews Apart." Tradition and Discovery: The Polanyi Society Periodical 33, no. 2 (2006): 8–24.

Nash, Ronald H. Life's Ultimate Questions: An Introduction to Philosophy. Grand Rapids: Zondervan, 1999.

———. The Concept of God. Contemporary evangelical perspectives.

Grand Rapids: Zondervan Pub. House, 1983.

———. The Light of the Mind: St. Augustine's Theory of Knowledge. Lexington, Kent.: The University Press of Kentucky, 1969.

Pabst, Adrian. Metaphysics: The Creation of Hierarchy. Interventions. Grand Rapids: Eerdmans, 2012.

Panaccio, Claude. Ockham on Concepts. Ashgate Studies in Medieval Philosophy. Burlington: Ashgate, 2004.

Pelletier, Jenny. William Ockham on Metaphysics: The Science of Being and God. Studien Und Texte Zur Geistesgeschichte Des Mittelalters. Leiden: Brill, 2013.

Polanyi, Michael. "Knowing and Being." In Knowing and Being : Essays by Michael Polanyi, edited by Marjorie Grene, 123–137. Chicago: University of Chicago Press, 1969.

———. Personal Knowledge: Towards a Post-Critical Philosophy. First Harper Torchbook Edition. New York: Harper Torchbook, 1964.

———. The Tacit Dimension. Chicago; London: University of Chicago Press, 2009.

Poythress, Vern S. In the Beginning Was the Word: Language: A God-Centered Approach. Wheaton: Crossway Books, 2009.

———. Logic: A God-Centered Approach to the Foundation of Western Thought. Electronic. Wheaton: Crossway, 2013.

———. "Reforming Ontology and Logic in the Light of the Trinity: An Application of Van Til's Idea of Analogy." Westminster Theological Journal 57 (1995): 187–219.

———. Symphonic Theology: The Validity of Multiple Perspectives in Theology. Grand Rapids: Academie Books, 1987.

Radde-Gallwitz, Andrew. Basil of Caesarea, Gregory of Nyssa, and the Transformation of Divine Simplicity. Oxford early Christian studies. Oxford; New York: Oxford University Press, 2009.

Rickless, Samuel C. "Berkeley's Treatise Concerning the Principles of Human Knowledge." In The Bloomsbury Companion to Berkeley, edited by Bertil Belfrage and Richard Brook. Bloomsbury Companions. New York: Bloomsbury Academic, 2017.

Rushdoony, Rousas John. "The One and the Many Problem—The Contribution of Van Til." In Jerusalem and Athens: Critical

Discussions on the Theology and Apologetics of Cornelius Van Til, edited by E. R. Geehan. USA: Presbyterian and Reformed, 1971.

Rutherford, J. Alexander. God's Kingdom through His Priest-King: An Analysis of the Book of Samuel in Light of the Davidic Covenant. Teleioteti Technical Studies 1. Vancouver: Teleioteti, 2019.

———. Prevenient Grace: An Investigation into Arminianism. 2nd Revised Ed. Teleioteti Technical Studies 2. Vancouver: Teleioteti, 2020.

———. Revelation, Retribution, and Reminder: A Biblical Exposition of the Doctrine of Hell. Airdrie, AB: Teleioteti, 2021.

Sickler, Bradley L. God on the Brain: What Cognitive Science Does (and Does Not) Tell Us about Faith, Human Nature, and the Divine. Wheaton, Illinois: Crossway, 2020.

Silva, Moisés. Biblical Words and Their Meaning: An Introduction to Lexical Semantics. Rev. and Expanded ed. Grand Rapids: Zondervan, 1994.

Ska, Jean Louis. "Our Fathers Have Told Us": Introduction to the Analysis of Hebrew Narratives. Subsidia Biblica 13. Roma: Editrice Pontificio Instituto Biblico, 1990.

Spade, Paul Vincent. "Ockham's Nominalist Metaphysics: Some Main Themes." In The Cambridge Companion to Ockham, edited by Paul Vincent Spade. Cambridge Companions to Philosophy. Cambridge: Cambridge Univ. Press, 1999.

Steven B. Cowan and James S. Spiegel. Idealism and Christian Philosophy : Idealism and Christianity Volume 2. Idealism and Christianity. New York: Bloomsbury Academic, 2016.

Stoneham, Tom. "Three Dialogues between Hylas, Philonous and the Sceptic." In The Bloomsbury Companion to Berkeley, edited by Bertil Belfrage and Richard Brook, 121–140. Bloomsbury Companions. New York: Bloomsbury Academic, 2017.

Van Til, Cornelius. A Christian Theory of Knowledge. Philadelphia: Presbyterian and Reformed Pub Co., 1969.

———. An Introduction to Systematic Theology. In Defense of the Faith V. Presbyterian and Reformed Pub. Co., 1974.

———. The Defense of the Faith. Edited by K. Scott Oliphint. 4th ed. Phillipsburg: P & R Pub, 2008.

Webster, John. "What Makes Theology Theological?" In God Without Measure: Working Papers in Christian Theology. Vol. I. T&T Clark Theology. London ; New York: Bloomsbury T&T Clark, 2016.

Welch, Edward T. Blame It on the Brain? Distinguishing Chemical Imbalances, Brain Disorders, and Disobedience. Resources for changing lives. Phillipsburg: P & R Pub, 1998.

Zachhuber, Johannes. The Rise of Christian Theology and the End of Ancient Metaphysics: Patristic Philosophy from the Cappadocian Fathers to John of Damascus. Oxford University Press, 2020.

Zentall, Thomas R., Edward A. Wasserman, Olga F. Lazareva, Roger K. R. Thompson, and Mary Jo Rattermann. "Concept Learning in Animals." Comparative Cognition & Behavior Reviews 3 (2008).

ABOUT TELEIOTETI

Teleioteti (Τελειοτητι, te-ley-o-tey-tee)—meaning "unto maturity"—is dedicated to faithful, thoughtful ministry. We create resources for Christian discipleship, resources that address theological and pastoral concerns from a biblical worldview. Our purpose is to see Christ's Church mature in its understanding of God and his Word. We do this through the production of Gospel-centred materials that connect the Bible with the heads, hearts, and minds of Christians. We hope to enable Christians from all walks of life to better understand and glorify God through service in his Church.

To achieve this purpose, Teleioteti publishes online materials and books researched with academic rigour yet based upon biblical presuppositions. That is, we are neither academic nor lazy. We use methods, or epistemology, informed by the Bible along with the hard work usually associated with professional research and study. We produce resources directed towards all Christians, but most of our resources are directed towards students, pastors, and theologically inclined lay Christians.

To learn more about us and what we are doing, please visit us at https://teleioteti.ca or contact us at info@teleioteti.ca. If you have found this resource helpful, prayerfully consider supporting us by giving a review on the web (e.g. Amazon, Goodreads, etc.), praying with and for us, or giving financially so that we can produce more resources like this one. For more information on how you can support us, visit us at https://teleioteti.ca/about/partner/.

Other Books by J. Alexander Rutherford

Other books in this series, "God's Gifts for the Christian Life" include the other 2 volumes of Part 1 – The Christian Mind and *The Gift of Purpose*, the first volume of Part 3 – The Christian Life. For all of our books, visit Teleioteti.ca. For upcoming books, see our page, Teleioteti.ca/coming-soon/.

Believe the Unbelievable: A Study in the Book of Habakkuk (Teleioteti, 2018)

What would we do if our prayers for justice, our prayers that God's will be done in our nation, were answered with a vision of desolation, of utter destruction?

When Habakkuk prayed for salvation, a prayer for justice in the midst of chaos, violence, and suffering, that was God's answer. He revealed in a vision the invasion of the vicious armies of Babylon. God's answer contradicted everything Habakkuk thought he knew. Yet in the end, he praised God and trusted him for this horrid salvation.

What do we do when God's actions or words contradict our understanding, contradict what we have believed? The book of Habakkuk answers this question in the face of the Babylonian invasion of Judah. Habakkuk is a book of discipleship, a book written to bring its reader to a deeper faith in Yahweh in the presence of his unthinkable deeds.

Using study questions addressing the text, theology, and application of Habakkuk and explanatory comments on difficult themes, *Believe the Unbelievable* seeks to realize this purpose for the contemporary reader.

Endorsements:

James Rutherford is a capable and creative thinker, well equipped to tackle tough projects, such as the book of Habakkuk. In this study guide, Rutherford has produced a very useful resource for individual or group study. He combines theological acumen and well-honed linguistic and literary skills to discover and then to present, in highly understandable fashion, the riches of this not so "minor" Minor Prophet.

- V. Philips Long, PhD Cambridge
  Professor of Old Testament, Regent College

My good friend, James Rutherford, has given the church a gift. He has taken his love for God's Word and focused it on an Old Testament book that most Christians know very little about. The result is a study in Habakkuk that brings together deep insight and real relevance. Habakkuk is a voice among the biblical chorus that believers need to hear today. Thank you, James, for helping us to hear it clearly and faithfully.

- Fredrick Eaton
  Pastor, Christ City Church, Kitsilano

Prevenient Grace: An Investigation into Arminianism – 2nd Revised Edition (Teleioteti, 2020)

When a building is built on a poor foundation, the inevitable result is its collapse. But this isn't a book on architecture; foundations are found in thought structures as well as in material structures. In theology, a bad foundation will produce results as catastrophic as a bad foundation in architecture. How we think about God and his work in the world will profoundly affect how we live and work out our Christian faith; is your foundation strong? This book evolved from the conviction that a prominent theological system rests on a fragile foundation.

Endorsements:

This book is a fine piece of scholarship. Rutherford presents his arguments with admirable clarity. His intention is to offer guidance for pastors and teachers who may be faced with questions about whether human beings have the freedom to accept or reject God. The great strength of Rutherford's book is his knowledge of biblical texts and an appropriate interpretation of them. He successfully shows that the claims of Arminianism with its view that prevenient grace allows an acceptance or rejection of God are not supported by biblical texts. Nor are they justified by philosophical arguments. They layout of the book and its careful treatment of arguments both for and against prevenient grace is a model of excellent writing. His chapters are supplemented by a Glossary that explains all specific terms and Appendices where detailed theological discussions are given. Most helpful is his Index of Scripture passages discussed.

- Dr. Shirley Sullivan
  FRSC (elected), Professor Emeritus of Classics, University of British Columbia

CPSIA information can be obtained
at www.ICGtesting.com
Printed in the USA
BVHW030550150921
616751BV00006B/809

9 781989 560198